Eyes Open 1

WORKBOOK
with Digital Pack

Vicki Anderson with Eoin Higgins

Contents

Starter Unit

Greetings

1 ★ **Complete the conversation with the phrases in the box.**

> What's your name?   Hi!   Nice to meet you   I'm

Greg: Hello!
Alice: ¹_____
Greg: I'm Greg. ²_____
Alice: ³_____ Alice.
Greg: Nice to meet you.
Alice: ⁴_____ , too!

The alphabet

2 ★ **Add the missing letters to the alphabet.**

Numbers

3 ★★ **Write the numbers as words from big to small.**

one hundred

_____

Time

4 ★★ **Label the clock with the phrases in the box.**

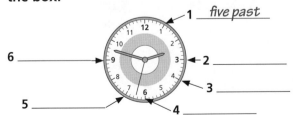

1 _five past_
2 _____
3 _____
4 _____
5 _____
6 _____

> a quarter past   five past   half past
> a quarter to   twenty past   twenty-five to

5 ★★★ Write the times.

1 _It's half past ten._
2 _____
3 _____
4 _____
5 _____
6 _____

Prepositions

6 ★ **Look at the pictures. Complete the sentences with the words in the box.**

> behind   in   in front of   between   next to   ~~on~~

1 The mouse is ___*on*___ the television.

2 The pizza is _____ the football and the television.

3 The bus is _____ the taxi.

4 The pizza is _____ the burger.

5 The taxi is _____ the bus.

6 The football is _____ the taxi.

Starter Unit

Classroom objects

1 ★★ Look at the pictures and complete the crossword.

across

down

this, that, these and those

2 ★★★ Write sentences for pictures 1–6.

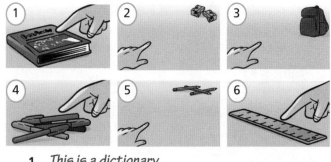

1   *This is a dictionary.*
2   _____
3   _____
4   _____
5   _____
6   _____

Possessive adjectives and possessive pronouns

3 ★ Circle the correct word.

1   'Where are **my** / mine rollerblades, Mum?'
    'They're in **your** / yours bedroom, Jenny!'
2   That car is **my** / **mine**.
3   Here are **your** / **yours** shoes, Ben.
4   Patricia and Amanda are at **their** / **theirs** house in the mountains.
5   This isn't **your** / **yours** pen. It's **her** / **hers**.
6   Is this book **our** / **ours** or **their** / **theirs**?

4 ★★ Write the correct possessive adjectives in the text.

Class 1C blog

Here are the photos of ¹_____ *our* _____ *class with* ²_____ *favourite things.*

Esma with ³_____ cat, Chester.

Alicia and ⁴_____ favourite books – the *Hunger Games* series.

Richard and Danny with ⁵_____ football shirts. Danny is Yeovil and Richard is Manchester United.

Colin's photo is unusual. It's ⁶_____ collection of insects!

Henry with ⁷_____ electric guitar.

And this photo is me, Bill, with ⁸_____ games console.

POSTED AT 12:25   COMMENT   SHARE

Starter Unit

Personal possessions and adjectives

1 ★★ **Write the adjectives and personal possessions.**

1 An e _xpensive_ l _aptop_

2 A n_____ s_____

3 An o_____ m_____ p_____

4 A b_____ b_____

5 A s_____ b_____

6 A n_____ c_____

Possessive 's

2 ★★ **Complete the sentences. Use the information from the class blog in Exercise 4 on page 4.**

1 _____Bill's_____ favourite thing is _____his_____ games console.

2 _____ favourite things are _____ insects.

3 Richard and _____ favourite things are _____ football shirts.

4 _____ favourite things are _____ books.

5 _____ favourite thing is _____ electric guitar.

6 _____ favourite thing is _____ cat, Chester.

be: affirmative, negative and questions

3 ★ **Look at the pictures and match the sentence beginnings and endings.**

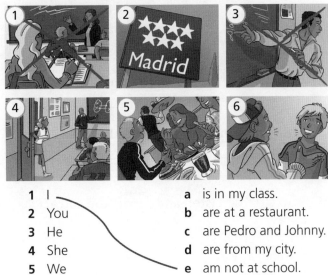

1 I
2 You
3 He
4 She
5 We
6 They

a is in my class.
b are at a restaurant.
c are Pedro and Johnny.
d are from my city.
e am not at school.
f isn't my teacher.

4 ★★★ **Write questions for the sentences you made in Exercise 3.**

1 _Am I at school?_____
2 _____
3 _____
4 _____
5 _____
6 _____

Days of the week

5 ★ **Find the seven days of the week in the wordsquare.**

Z	E	H	Y	U	K	P	X	H	G	N	U
M	V	J	G	F	N	E	J	Z	A	D	R
T	H	U	R	S	D	A	Y	R	T	E	Q
G	T	L	V	B	M	X	P	C	U	M	R
S	F	Q	T	U	O	E	D	X	E	H	M
A	H	D	G	T	N	C	R	R	S	Z	H
T	Y	S	U	N	D	A	Y	V	D	F	T
U	O	L	P	B	A	U	M	L	A	R	W
R	M	S	W	O	Y	I	N	K	Y	I	E
D	E	S	F	D	B	V	U	I	O	D	K
A	C	Y	I	U	T	E	A	F	Y	A	L
Y	B	W	E	D	N	E	S	D	A	Y	F

Starter Unit

Months and dates

1 ★ **Put the letters in order to make months.**

1 anJuyra
_____January_____

2 uyarbeFr
_____

3 lirpA
_____

4 guAtsu
_____

5 emetbrpeS
_____

6 cOtbroe
_____

7 removeNb
_____

8 ermecDeb
_____

2 ★★ **Which months are not in Exercise 1?**

_____ _____

_____ _____

3 ★★ 🔊 `01` **Listen and ⟨circle⟩ the correct dates.**

1 ⟨October 1⟩ / 31
2 February 5 / 15
3 April 8 / 18
4 September 3 / 30
5 January 22 / June 22
6 May 10 / March 10
7 December 25 / November 25
8 August 5 / July 5

4 ★★★ 🔊 `02` **Listen and write the dates.**

1 _January 6_
2 _____
3 _____
4 _____
5 _____
6 _____

Countries, nationalities and languages

5 ★ **Match the countries with the languages.**

1 Japan
2 Brazil
3 Australia
4 Morocco
5 Poland
6 Colombia

a English
b Polish
c Spanish
d Japanese
e Portuguese
f Arabic

6 ★★ **Write the nationalities.**

1 Maria Sharapova's from Russia.
She's _Russian_

2 Justin Bieber's from Canada. He's _____ .

3 Nicole Kidman's from Australia.
She's _____ .

4 Robert Pattinson's from the UK.
He's _____ .

5 Cristiano Ronaldo's from Portugal.
He's _____ .

6 Lady Gaga's from the USA. She's _____ .

7 ★★★ **Complete the sentences about the famous people. Use the Internet to find the information.**

1 Rihanna is from _the USA_ . She's an
American singer. Her language is _English_

2 Neymar and Kaká are footballers from
_____ . They are _____ football
players. Their first language is _____ .

3 Antonio Banderas is an actor from _____ .
He speaks _____ and _____ .

4 Simon Baker, the actor in *The Mentalist*, is from
_____ . He's a Hollywood actor in America,
but he's not _____ .

5 Agnieszka Radwańska is a tennis player from
_____ . Her first language is _____ .

Speaking review

8 ★ **Complete the conversation with the words in the box.**

repeat   course   spell   ~~right~~   Sorry

A: So, your first name is Alex, ¹_____right_____ ?
B: Yes, that's right.
A: And what's your surname?
B: Gallagher.
A: ²_____ ? Can you ³_____ that, please?
B: Yes, of ⁴_____ . It's Gallagher.
A: How do you ⁵_____ that?
B: G-A-L-L-A-G-H-E-R.

1 People

Vocabulary

Family and friends

1 ★ **Find 11 more words for people in your life in the wordsquare.**

t	e	a	m	m	a	t	e	b	u	n	g
e	c	o	u	s	i	n	o	r	n	e	r
a	r	c	n	o	n	a	h	o	c	p	a
m	g	l	d	a	p	p	c	t	l	g	n
x	r	a	p	d	f	y	x	h	e	t	d
c	a	s	y	m	a	r	r	e	l	a	d
a	n	s	i	s	t	e	r	r	a	n	a
u	d	m	z	t	h	n	s	g	o	d	d
n	m	a	k	l	e	t	m	u	m	d	h
t	a	t	i	a	b	g	s	n	l	a	n
x	b	e	s	t	f	r	i	e	n	d	r

2 ★★ **Complete the sentences. Use words from Exercise 1.**

1 My mother's father is my ___granddad___ .
2 Your aunt's son is your _____ .
3 The other people in his football team are his

   _____ .
4 Her dad's brother is her _____ .
5 My class teacher's students are my

   _____ .
6 Your favourite person to be with is your

   _____ .

3 ★★★ **Complete the sentences with 's and a family word.**

1 My dad _'s mum___ is my grandma.
2 My sister _____ is my dad.
3 My mum _____ is my aunt.
4 My cousin _____ is my uncle.
5 My mum _____ is my grandma.
6 My dad _____ is my granddad.

4 ★★ **Look at the family tree. Write the correct family words.**

Marta Ignacio

Angel Alicia Manuel Elena

Eric Me! Ana Gabriel Elisa

1 Ana is my ___sister___ .
2 Gabriel and Elisa are my _____ .
3 Elena is my _____ .
4 Marta is my _____ .
5 Alicia is my _____ .
6 Eric is my _____ .
7 Manuel is my _____ .
8 Ignacio is my _____ .

5 ★★★ **Draw your family tree and add names. Write at least five sentences about your family.**

Jane and Katie are my cousins.

Language focus 1

have got: affirmative and negative

1 ★ (Circle) the correct words in the grammar table.

1	I, You, We, They **have / has** got brown hair.
2	He, She, It **have / has** got green eyes.
3	I, You, We, They **haven't / hasn't** got red hair.
4	He, She, It **haven't / hasn't** got blue eyes.

2 ★ (Circle) the correct words.

I ¹ **('ve got)** / **'s got** a big family. I ² **'ve got** / **'s got** one brother and two sisters. My brother ³ **'ve got** / **'s got** a girlfriend. My parents ⁴ **has got** / **have got** a lot of brothers and sisters, so we ⁵ **'ve got** / **'s got** twelve cousins – all boys! We ⁶ **haven't got** / **hasn't got** a big house, so for family parties everyone visits our grandparents. They ⁷ **'s got** / **'ve got** a great house for parties!

3 ★★ Write the correct form of *have got* in the sentences.

1 We **_'ve got_** (✓) 120,000 hairs on our head.
2 You _____ (✗) a mobile phone. No problem! Tom Cruise _____ (✗) a mobile phone OR a computer.
3 Cristiano Ronaldo _____ (✗) one car. He _____ (✓) 18 cars at the moment!
4 I _____ (✓) blue eyes but my mum and dad _____ (✗) blue eyes. Their eyes are brown. My grandma _____ (✓) blue eyes.

have got: questions and short answers

4 ★ (Circle) the correct word for each question. Match the questions with the answers.

1 (Have) / Has you and I got a mobile phone?
2 Have / Has your grandparents got a car?
3 Have / Has Paris got a metro?
4 Have / Has you got a bike?
5 Have / Has Lady Gaga got blue eyes?
6 Have / Has Marc Gasol got a sister?

a Yes, it has.
b No, he hasn't.
c Yes, I have.
d Yes, we have.
e No, they haven't.
f No, she hasn't.

5 ★★ Complete the question about each picture. Write the correct answer.

1 A: ____*Have*____ you got fair hair?
   B: ____*No, I haven't.*____

2 A: _____ they _____ curly hair?
   B: _____

3 A: _____ we _____ a dog?
   B: _____

4 A: _____ your cousin _____ long, dark hair?
   B: _____

Explore adjectives

6 ★★ (Circle) the correct words.

1 Lionel Messi is a footballer. He's very (**good**) / **bad**.
2 I'm from Russia. It's a very **big / small** country.
3 Your English is very good. You're **lucky / unlucky**.
4 This is my new mobile phone. I love it! I'm really **happy / unhappy** with it!
5 Shhh! Be **quiet / noisy**!

7 ★★★ Complete the sentences with the opposite of the adjectives in the box with *un-*.

tidy	~~happy~~	healthy	usual

1 Poor Bob! He's really **_unhappy_** because he doesn't understand!
2 Wow! Your shoes are very _____ – they're yellow and blue.
3 This is my bedroom. It's very _____ . Sorry.
4 Burgers are very _____ .

Listening and vocabulary

Describing people

1 ★ **Match the pictures with the descriptions.**

1 spiky, fair hair ___

2 long, dark hair ___

3 short, curly hair ___

2 ★★ **Look at the pictures below. Complete the sentences with the words in the box.**

> fair tall short (x3) ~~dark~~
> brown long curly

1 Usain Bolt (1 m 95) is tall and he's got short,
   ___dark___ hair.
2 Jack Black (1 m 68) is short and he's got short,
   _____ hair.
3 Maria Sharapova (1 m 88) is _____ .
   She's got _____ , fair hair.
4 Neymar (1 m 75) is _____ . He's got short,
   _____ hair.
5 Shakira (1 m 55) is _____ . She's got long,
   _____ hair.
6 Javier Bardem (1 m 81) is tall. He's got
   _____ , dark hair.

Listening

3 ★★ 🔊 **03** **Listen to three teenagers talking about their families. Write *Owen*, *Connor* or *Jane* under the correct pictures.**

2 _____

1 _____   3 _____

4 ★ **Match the names with the information.**

1 Jane is …   a an identical twin.
2 Owen is …   b an only child.
3 Connor is …   c one of five brothers and sisters.

5 ★★★ 🔊 **03** **Listen again. Write *Jane*,**
***Connor* or *Owen*.**

1 ___Jane___ uses a computer to chat with friends.
2 _____ has got four sisters.
3 _____ has got a lot of cousins.
4 _____ has got a problem with the
   bathroom.
5 _____ likes a friend's house.
6 _____ is friends with his/her family.
7 _____ is a good student.

Usain Bolt

Jack Black

Maria Sharapova

Neymar

Shakira

Javier Bardem

Language focus 2

Comparative adjectives

1 ★★ **Complete the table with the comparative forms of the adjectives in the box.**

Form	Adjective	Comparative
1 syllable	old long dark short young	*older* 1 _____ 2 _____ 3 _____ 4 _____
1 syllable ending in single consonant	big red thin	*bigger* 5 _____ 6 _____
2+ syllables	intelligent beautiful	*more intelligent* 7 _____
2 syllables ending in -*y*	funny curly noisy pretty	*funnier* 8 _____ 9 _____ 10 _____
Irregular adjectives	good	11 _____

2 ★★★ **Write sentences about Joanna's family.**

1 My mother / short / curly hair / me
   My mother has shorter and curlier hair than me.

2 My father / old / my mother
   _____

3 My brother / young / me
   _____

4 I / tall / my father
   _____

5 My brother / funny / me and my dad
   _____

6 I / intelligent / my mother and father
   _____

7 My mother / thin / my father
   _____

8 My brother / good at / football / my dad
   _____

Explore adjective suffixes -*ful*

3 ★★★ **Complete the sentences with the adjective form of the words in the box.**

| ~~beauty~~ use wonder colour care |

1 What a ___*beautiful*___ cat! Is it yours?
2 Be _____ ! There's a car!
3 I like the *Hunger Games* books. They're
   _____ .
4 My new bike is yellow, red, blue and green! It's very _____ .
5 If you don't understand a word, here's a dictionary. It's very _____ .

Reading

1 ★ **Read the text about Ruby and Rachel. Answer the questions.**

1 Which is the correct picture?
2 Where are they from?
3 Where do they live?
4 What's their favourite hobby?

AM I RUBY OR RACHEL? ⊗

Ruby Taylor and Rachel Storr are very *unusual*. They are *identical twins*, but they've got different parents. The twins are from China, but they are adopted. They both live in Scotland, Ruby near Aberdeen, and Rachel in Edinburgh, 150 km away. In her Scottish family Rachel has got two brothers, but Ruby is an '*only child*'. Ruby often visits Rachel, and their parents are now friends.

Both girls have got two 'families': their parents, an 'aunt' and 'uncle' (the other twin's parents) and eight grandparents!

Rachel and Ruby have got long, dark hair and brown eyes. They aren't just identical, they are mirror-image twins. Rachel writes with her right hand and Ruby writes with her left hand, for example. Their favourite *hobby* is art and they both love clothes. Ruby wears Rachel's clothes and Rachel wears Ruby's clothes, and they play a game with their grandparents called 'Am I Ruby or am I Rachel?'. Their grandparents haven't got any idea!

2 ★★ **Write the words in *bold italics* from the text next to the definitions.**

1 A child with no brothers or sisters. An _____
2 Brothers or sisters who look the same and have the same birthday. _____
3 An interest. A _____
4 Very different or strange. _____

3 ★★ **Read the text again. Are these sentences true (*T*) or false (*F*)?**

1 Rachel and Ruby live in the same family. *F*
2 One of the twins lives in England. ____
3 They've got four grandmothers. ____
4 They've got the same hair and eyes. ____
5 Ruby and Rachel use the same hand to write. ____
6 They've got the same interests. ____
7 Their grandparents think the game that Rachel and Ruby play is easy. ____

4 ★★★ **Read the sentences and write *Ra* for Rachel, *Ru* for Ruby or *B* for both.**

1 She's from China. ____
2 She lives in Edinburgh. ____
3 She hasn't got any brothers or sisters. ____
4 She's got brown eyes. ____
5 She writes with her right hand. ____
6 She wears the other girl's clothes. ____

5 ★★★ **Why are Ruby and Rachel unusual? Find two or three things in the text. Write them down.**

> **READING TIP**
>
> If you see a word you don't know, don't stop reading. You don't need to know every word to understand a text. If you continue reading, sometimes you can understand the new word.

Writing

A description of a person

1 **Read the description. What is Shakira's hobby?**

My favourite singer is **Shakira**. She's 37 years old and she's from Colombia. She's got brown eyes and quite long, wavy fair hair. She's not very tall but she's very pretty. She's also very intelligent. She speaks Spanish, English, Italian, Arabic and Portuguese!

Shakira is a singer and she's got a lot of prizes for her music. But she's also a really amazing dancer. Her husband is the FC Barcelona footballer Gerard Pique and they've got the same birthday, 3 February. They've also got a son called Milan. Her hobby is collecting rings – she's got over 200 of them. She's also got two organisations that help children. I love Shakira!

2 **Read the description again. Answer the questions.**

1 What nationality is Shakira?

_____

2 How many languages does she speak?

_____

3 When is her birthday?

_____

4 What's her son's name?

_____

5 How many organisations does she have?

_____

Useful language Modifiers ────────

3 **Read the description again. Which words go before these adjectives?**

1 _____ long
2 _____ tall
3 _____ pretty
4 _____ intelligent
5 _____ amazing

4 **Put the words in the correct order to make phrases.**

1 very / girl / a / pretty
   A very pretty girl.

2 intelligent / really / woman / a
   _____

3 really / footballer / a / amazing
   _____

4 hair / not very / long
   _____

5 funny / he's / quite
   _____

5 **Write five sentences about people you know with the modifiers in A and the adjectives in B.**

A

| not very | quite | really | very |

B

| long | tall | young | pretty | intelligent | funny |

1 *My friend Carolina has got quite long hair.*
2 _____
3 _____
4 _____
5 _____
6 _____

Writing

> **WRITING TIP**
>
> **Make it better! ✓ ✓ ✓**
> Use *and* to join sentences and before the last thing in a list.
> *I like cheese, tomatoes **and** pasta.*
> *My sister is tall **and** she has got long hair.*

6 **Join sentences 1–3 with *and*. Then put *and* in sentences 4–6.**

1 My brother likes football. He goes swimming.
My brother likes football and swimming.

2 My dad is very tall. He is very funny.
_____

3 My friend has got a dog. He's got a cat.
_____

4 He likes basketball, tennis, music.
_____

5 My mum speaks French, German, Spanish.
_____

6 She's got long hair, big blue eyes, a brown hat.
_____

7 **Complete the sentences with *he's* or *he's got*.**

1 _____ quite tall with short hair.
2 _____ not very young but _____ very good at football.
3 _____ dark brown eyes.
4 _____ two brothers and one sister.
5 _____ very good-looking and funny.
6 _____ a very expensive laptop.

> **WRITING TIP**
>
> **Make it better! ✓ ✓ ✓**
> Write interesting facts about the person in your description.

8 **Read the description of Shakira again. Find interesting facts about her.**

9 **Look again at Exercise 1. Put the headings in the same order as the information in the text.**

| where the person is from   relationships   age |
| favourite things   ~~name~~   physical appearance |

1 ___name___   4 _____
2 _____   5 _____
3 _____   6 _____

PLAN

10 **Make notes about a person you know or someone famous. Use the headings in Exercise 9.**

WRITE

11 **Write a description of the person in Exercise 10. Look at page 19 of the Student's Book to help you.**

_____
_____
_____
_____
_____
_____
_____
_____
_____
_____
_____
_____

CHECK

12 **Check your writing. Can you say YES to the questions?**

- Is the information from Exercise 9 in your description?
- Is there something interesting about the person in your description?
- Are there modifiers before the adjectives?
- Are the grammar, spelling and punctuation correct?

Do you need to write a second draft?

Vocabulary
Family and friends

1 Look at Kathy's family tree. Label it with the words in the box.

> dad   uncle (x2)   grandma   granddad   aunt (x2)   brother   cousin (x3)   mum   sister

Kathy (me)

1 _____
2 _____
3 _____
4 _____
5 _____
6 _____
7 _____
8 _____
9 _____
10 _____
11 _____
12 _____
13 _____

Total: 13

Describing people

2 Complete the sentences with the words in the box.

> blue   old   short   spiky   ~~tall~~   fair

1 Cassandra isn't short. She's ____*tall*____ .
2 She isn't young. She's _____ .
3 Her hair isn't long. It's _____ .
4 Her hair isn't curly. It's _____ .
5 Her eyes aren't green. They're _____ .
6 Her hair isn't _____ . It's dark.

Total: 5

Language focus
have got: affirmative and negative

3 Look at the table. Complete the sentences with the correct form of *have got*. Use contracted forms if possible.

	Luke	Sally
brothers	2	0
sisters	1	2
pets	0	1 dog
computer	1	1
mobile phone	1	1

Luke ¹____*'s got*____ two brothers. He ²_____ one sister. He ³_____ a pet.

Sally ⁴_____ a brother. She ⁵_____ two sisters. She ⁶_____ a dog.

Luke and Sally ⁷_____ computers and they ⁸_____ mobile phones.

Total: 7

Comparative adjectives

4 **Write the comparative form of the adjectives.**

1 young   _younger_
2 old   _____
3 curly   _____
4 intelligent   _____
5 good   _____
6 funny   _____
7 tall   _____
8 noisy   _____
9 long   _____
10 quiet   _____

Total: 9

Language builder

5 **Choose the correct option.**

My family's not big and it's not small. I ¹ _'ve got_ two sisters. ² _____ names are Holly and Lola. They're both ³ _____ than me. Holly's got long, straight hair and she ⁴ _____ really funny. Her favourite thing is ⁵ _____ skateboard. Lola's got short brown hair and she's very intelligent. Her favourite thing is her laptop. My dad ⁶ _____ brothers or sisters but my mum's got one sister. Her name's Olive. She's got one son. ⁷ _____ name's Michael. Michael ⁸ _____ favourite thing is his bike. He's younger ⁹ _____ us and he's noisier than ¹⁰ _____ too!

1 a 's got   b ('ve got)
2 a Our   b Their
3 a older   b more old
4 a are   b is
5 a her   b hers
6 a haven't got   b hasn't got
7 a Its   b His
8 a 's   b s'
9 a more   b than
10 a ours   b us

Total: 9

Vocabulary builder

6 **Circle the correct option.**

1 My cousin is four years old. She's very old / (young)
2 My father's brother is my aunt / uncle.
3 His brother's hair is short and spiky / good-looking.
4 My mum's parents are my grandparents / cousins.
5 Louise has got fair / brown eyes.
6 Our teacher's very tall / curly.
7 My brother's / sister's name is Tom.
8 London is in Britain / British.
9 My dad's wife is my mum / uncle.
10 My mum's sister is my aunt / uncle.
11 My uncle's son is my cousin / sister.
12 My classmate's hair is very tall / straight.

Total: 11

Speaking

7 **Complete the phone conversation with the words in the box.**

> Just a minute.   Hello?
> Can I call you back?   Hi, it's Katie.

Max: ¹ _____
Katie: ² _____ How are you?
Max: Hi Katie. I'm fine thanks. You?
Katie: I'm OK thanks. Have you got Colin's email address?
Max: Yes, I have. It's on my phone. ³ _____ I've got it now. It's colinfrench@netmail.com
Katie: Great. Thanks. I've got a question about our science homework.
Max: Sorry, but I haven't got time at the moment. ⁴ _____
Katie: Sure. Speak in an hour?
Max: Great. Bye.
Katie: Bye.

Total: 4

Total: 58

15

have got

Remember that:

- we use *have* / *'ve* with *I, you, they, we*
- we use *has* / *'s* with *he, she, it*
- we always use *got* after *have* in affirmative and negative sentences and in questions
- we don't use *got* after *have* in short answers

1 Find and correct five more mistakes in the conversation.

Simon: Hi, Lara, have you ˄a big family?
got

Lara: No, I haven't. My family is small. I not got brothers or sisters.

Simon: Have you got a dog?

Lara: Yes, I has and I love him! He's got curly brown hair and he's very funny. I play with him every day.

Simon: Have your house got a garden?

Lara: Yes, it has. It's really beautiful. You have got time to visit me?

Simon: No, I haven't got. I've got homework!

Spell it right! Adjectives

Remember that:

- we never add *s* to adjectives when we describe more than one thing
  two ~~news~~ mobile phones → *two new mobile phones*
- adjectives with *-ful* have only one *l*.
  It's a ~~wonderfull~~ time! → *It's a **wonderful** time!*

2 Are the sentences correct? Correct the incorrect sentences.

1 She's got one younger sister and two olders brothers.
   She's got one younger sister and two older brothers.

2 His bedroom is very colourfull and tidy.
   _____

3 We go to the same school but we've got different teachers.
   _____

4 Dictionaries are very usefuls books.
   _____

5 She's got blues eyes and red hair.
   _____

6 Kim and Julie are my favourite cousins. They're identical twins.
   _____

7 The twins wear unusuals clothes and they've got beautifull hair.
   _____

8 The parties at my grandparents' house are wonderfuls!
   _____

Comparative adjectives

Remember that:

- we double the consonant at the end of adjectives with one syllable
  ~~biger~~ → bigger
- we take away the *y* and add *-ier* to the end of adjectives that end in *y*
  ~~noisyer~~ → noisier
- we use *more* + adjective with two or more syllables. We don't use *more* + adjective + *-er*
  ~~more beautifuler~~ → more beautiful

3 Complete the text with the correct form of the adjectives in brackets.

My sister is older and ¹___*thinner*___ (thin) than me and she's got longer hair than me. It's ²_____ (curly) and ³_____ (red) too. I also think she's ⁴_____ (pretty) than me. But my friends think she isn't. Her clothes are ⁵_____ (dark) than mine and she's better at netball than me. I think she's ⁶_____ (intelligent) than me, too. But I'm funnier than her and I think I'm happier than her. She hasn't got a lot of friends.

2 It's your life

Vocabulary

Daily routines

1 ★ Use the clues to complete the crossword.

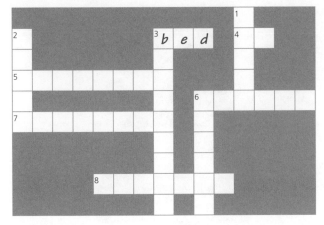

across

3 go to _____

4 get _____

5 do some _____

6 go to _____

7 do my _____

8 get _____

down

1 have _____

2 brush my _____

3 have _____

6 have a _____

2 ★ Complete the text about Victor's daily routine.

Hi. My name's Victor. I'm 13. I live at La Masia, part of Football Club Barcelona. People think we play football all day but it's not true. This is our daily routine:
At 6.45 we ¹g*et*_____ u*p*_____ and ²g_____ d_____ . At 7.00 we ³h_____ b_____ – we eat a lot!
    We go to school on a bus at 7.30. We ⁴g_____ t_____ s_____ at 8.00 and we finish classes at 2.00. We ⁵h_____ l_____ at 2.15. At 3.00 in the afternoon we've got a free hour. I chat with friends or sleep. At 4.00 we ⁶d_____ our h_____ or we've got extra classes. From 6.50 to 8.45 we ⁷d_____ s_____ e_____ in the sports hall or we've got football training. After training we ⁸h_____ a s_____ and then we have dinner at 9.30. After that we've got TV, games or the Internet and at 11.00 we ⁹g_____ t_____ b_____ . It's a long day!

3 ★★★ Is your daily routine similar to Victor's? Write sentences to compare your routine with Victor's.

Victor gets up at 6.45. I get up at …

4 ★★ Write at least five other activities you do after school or at the weekend. Use a dictionary if necessary.

Language focus 1

Present simple: affirmative and negative

1 ★ (Circle) the correct words in the grammar table.

1	I, You, We, They **go / goes** to the cinema.
2	He, She, It **finish / finishes** at six o'clock.
3	I, You, We, They **don't study / doesn't study** music.
4	He, She, It **don't eat / doesn't eat** a lot.

2 ★★ Complete the texts with the correct form of the verbs in brackets.

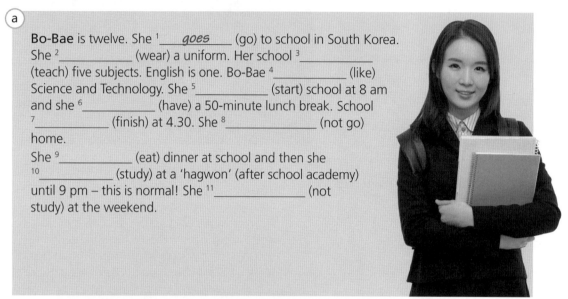

a

Bo-Bae is twelve. She ¹____*goes*____ (go) to school in South Korea. She ²_____ (wear) a uniform. Her school ³_____ (teach) five subjects. English is one. Bo-Bae ⁴_____ (like) Science and Technology. She ⁵_____ (start) school at 8 am and she ⁶_____ (have) a 50-minute lunch break. School ⁷_____ (finish) at 4.30. She ⁸_____ (not go) home.
She ⁹_____ (eat) dinner at school and then she ¹⁰_____ (study) at a 'hagwon' (after school academy) until 9 pm – this is normal! She ¹¹_____ (not study) at the weekend.

b

Elias and Paul are eleven. They ¹____*go*____ (go) to a secondary school in Germany. They ²_____ (not wear) a uniform. They ³_____ (study) English, Latin and 13 other subjects. They ⁴_____ (start) school at 7.30 and ⁵_____ (finish) classes at 1.30 pm. Elias and Paul ⁶_____ (not have) lunch at school. They ⁷_____ (eat) at Paul's house with his family. Elias's parents ⁸_____ (work) all day. After lunch, Paul and Elias ⁹_____ (play) sports or games or ¹⁰_____ (do) their homework. They ¹¹_____ (love) their school!

(E)xplore prepositions of time

3 ★ (Circle) the correct words.
1 (On) / At Monday.
2 In / At 7 o'clock.
3 In / At June.
4 At / On night.
5 In / At the weekend.
6 In / On the morning.

4 ★★ Complete the sentences with *in, on* or *at*.
1 We start school ____*at*____ 8.30.
2 They don't go to school _____ July.
3 Does she play tennis _____ lunchtime?
4 Sometimes I do my homework _____ night.
5 What do you do _____ the weekend?
6 My birthday is _____ 6 March.

5 ★★★ Complete the sentences with your own ideas.
1 At lunchtime at school I usually …
2 I never wake up … on Saturdays.
3 I always get dressed …
4 I usually have breakfast …
5 I always do my homework …

Listening and vocabulary

After school activities

1 ⭐ **Put the letters in order to make nine after school activities. Write them with the correct verbs.**

1 sucim
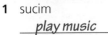
play music

2 netsin
_____

3 shecs
_____

4 gwinmism
_____

5 rat secsals
_____

6 ataker
_____

7 denac seaslsc
_____

8 lobtolfa
_____

9 ramad
_____

Listening

2 ⭐⭐ 🔊 04 **Listen to an interview with a young dancer, Noel Peters. Tick the correct sentences.**

a He works long days. ☐
b He goes to bed early. ☐
c He loves dancing. ☐

3 ⭐⭐ 🔊 04 **Listen again. Mark the sentences true (*T*) or false (*F*).**

1 He's got a tutor in the hotel. ___
2 Noel lives in New York for one week and at home for two weeks. ___
3 He's got the same routine in New York and at home. ___
4 He has a lot of free time. ___

4 ⭐⭐⭐ 🔊 04 **Listen again. Complete the times of Noel's daily routine.**

activity	New York	home
gets up	9.00	
has breakfast		
has lunch		
has dinner		
goes to bed		

Language focus 2

Present simple: *Yes/No* questions

1 ★ (Circle) the correct words in the grammar table.

1	Do / Does I, we, you, they speak English?
2	Yes, I, we, you, they do / does.
3	What time do I, we, you, they goes / go to bed?

2 ★★ Complete the questions with the words in brackets.

1 A: *Do you eat* a lot of vegetables? (you / eat)
   B: Yes, I do.
2 A: _____ the guitar? (your brother / play)
   B: No, he doesn't.
3 A: _____ school at 1.30? (Elias and Paul / finish)
   B: Yes, they do.
4 A: _____ chess? (you / like)
   B: No, I don't.
5 A: _____ to school in the evening? (Bo-Bae / go)
   B: Yes, she does.
6 A: _____ tennis at school? (you all / play)
   B: No, we don't.

3 ★★ Complete the short answers to the questions.

1 Do they play baseball in Cuba?
   Yes, they do.
2 Does school finish at two o'clock on Friday?
   No, _____ .
3 Do they have lunch at school?
   Yes, _____ .
4 Does Rafa Nadal live in Monaco?
   No, _____ .
5 Do you go to school on Saturday mornings?
   No, _____ .
6 Does your mother go swimming?
   Yes, _____ .

Present simple: *Wh-* questions

4 ★ (Circle) the correct words.

1 What (do) / does we wear in our new karate class?
2 Where do / does she want to go after school?
3 Who do / does I ask about after school activities?
4 What time do / does you usually get up?
5 When do / does the next class start?
6 Where do / does Lauren and Carla go to school?

Adverbs of frequency

5 ★ Write the adverbs of frequency in order.

| sometimes   usually   always   never   often |

100% 90%   75%   40%   0%

_____   _____   _____   *never*

6 ★★ Write present simple sentences with the prompts. Use adverbs of frequency.

1 Eric / play baseball / at the weekend (75%)
   Eric often plays baseball at the weekend.
2 I / be / quiet / at parties (90%)
   _____
3 Anna and Rebecca / be / late for class (0%)
   _____
4 We / go / to a restaurant / on Saturdays (40%)
   _____
5 Cati / do her homework / in bed (100%)
   _____
6 My cousins / visit us / in the holidays (75%)
   _____

Explore expressions with *have* 1

7 ★★ Complete the sentences with the words in the box.

| drink   shower   snack   dinner   breakfast |

1 I always have *breakfast* before I go to school.
2 After school, I usually have a sandwich for a _____ .
3 In the evening, I always have _____ with my family and then I go to bed.
4 I usually have a _____ of water after I play tennis.
5 When I get up in the morning I always have a _____ and brush my teeth.

8 ★★★ Write a response with the words in brackets.

1 A: What a great football game! I'm thirsty!
   B: *Why don't you have a drink* ? (have a drink)
2 A: What do you do when you wake up?
   B: _____ (have a shower)
3 A: Are you hungry?
   B: Yes! _____ ? (have a snack)
4 A: It's 7.30. I've got two pizzas.
   B: OK, _____ (have dinner)
5 A: What do you before you leave the house?
   B: _____ (have breakfast)

Reading

1 ★ **Read the text about after school activities. Write the activities for pictures 1–6.**

1 _____

2 _____

3 _____

4 _____

5 _____

6 _____

2 ★★ **Complete the sentences with the words in *bold italics* from the text.**

1 You go to a theatre to see a _____ .
2 _____ are something people try to win.
3 There are two or three _____ in a school year.
4 You have a _____ when people often meet to do an activity together.
5 You can go swimming in a _____ .
6 A person who plays music is a _____ .

3 ★★ **Read the text again and ⟲circle⟳ the correct options.**

1 Misaki goes to *juku* _b_ days a week.
  a three **ⓑ** four **c** five
2 Chloe has dance classes ___ .
  a two days a week **b** three times a week
  c at the end of term
3 Chloe doesn't ___ very well.
  a dance **b** write **c** draw
4 Mikko does ___ after school activities.
  a two **b** three **c** four
5 Mikko doesn't play ___ .
  a music **b** games **c** sports
6 Jorge does athletics ___ days a week.
  a two **b** three **c** four

4 ★★★ **Who says these sentences? Write *Misaki*, *Chloe*, *Mikko* or *Jorge*.**

1 'I can play *Happy Birthday* on the guitar.'
  _____
2 'The water is very cold!' _____
3 'The photos of the show are on my Facebook page.' _____
4 'Where are my running shoes?' _____
5 'My teacher has a concert tomorrow.'
  _____
6 'What colours can I use in my drawing?'

5 ★★★ **What extra school activities do you and your friends do? Write about your weekly routine.**

> **READING TIP** ....
>
> Ask your teacher or use a dictionary if you don't understand a word in a text and the words around it don't help.

A MISAKI, JAPAN

During the week, a lot of Japanese students go to *juku* (a homework **club**) after school. My friends and I go there three days a week and on Saturday morning. We learn Maths, Science and English. I also go swimming – my school has a big swimming **pool**.

B CHLOE, ENGLAND

I love dancing and when I finish school I have dance classes on Mondays and Wednesdays. At the end of the **term** we have a **show** – we dance in front of all our parents and friends. On Tuesdays and Thursdays I have Art classes. I'm not very good at drawing!

C MIKKO, FINLAND

I like playing music so I have music classes after school. I play the guitar and my teacher is a rock **musician**. I also play chess and our school has a chess club. We sometimes have **competitions** with other schools.

D JORGE, SPAIN

I have English classes after school every Tuesday and Thursday, but on the other days of the week, I do athletics. I love running and I want to go to the Olympic Games. I don't play other sports but my brother does karate.

Writing

A blog post

1 Read Mary's blog post. What does she do after school?

MY WEEK

I get up at 8.00 every morning. I have some breakfast and I walk to school with my friends Claire and Isabelle. I finish school at 2.30 in the afternoon but I don't always go home. On Mondays and Wednesdays, I play tennis after school. On Fridays, I go to dance classes. On the other days, I usually watch TV after I do my homework. Sometimes at the weekend Claire comes to my house and we play video games and talk about … well, everything! I have my dinner at about 7 o'clock but I don't always watch TV after dinner. It's very boring! Sometimes I read a book or chat online. I usually go to bed at about 9.30.

2 Read the blog again. When does Mary do these things?

1	get up	*8.00*
2	finish school	
3	play tennis	
4	go to dance class	
5	play video games with Claire	
6	have dinner	
7	go to bed	

3 Tick (✓) the things Mary does **not** do.
1 have breakfast ☐
2 walk to school ☐
3 always go home after school ☐
4 play video games ☐
5 always watch TV after dinner ☐

Useful language   Connectors ————

4 (Circle) the correct options.
After school, I do my homework ¹(and) / *but* I watch TV. We always have some homework ²*and* / *but* we don't always have a lot. I sometimes help my mum and dad with the dinner ³*and* / *but* I don't really know how to cook! After dinner I read a book ⁴*and* / *but* play the violin. I don't chat online ⁵*and* / *but* I send messages to my friends on my mobile phone.

5 Complete the daily activities with a word from the box.

> do (x2)   brush   have (x3)   go (x2)   get (x2)

1 ___*have*___ breakfast
2 _____ my teeth
3 _____ up
4 _____ a shower
5 _____ dressed
6 _____ to school
7 _____ my homework
8 _____ lunch
9 _____ to bed
10 _____ some exercise

Writing

6 Complete the sentences with _have_ or _have got_.

1 I _____ a shower before I go to school.
2 I _____ a very fast computer.
3 I _____ a lot of interesting books about Science.
4 I _____ lunch at school.
5 I always _____ breakfast before I go to school.

> **WRITING TIP**
>
> Make it better! ✓ ✓ ✓
> Use time expressions (_at 8 o'clock, before school, in the morning_) to say <u>when</u> you do things.
> _I have a shower **at 7.30**._

7 Complete the sentences about your daily activities with time expressions.

1 I get up _____ .
2 I do my homework _____ .
3 I have lunch _____ .
4 I have a shower _____ .
5 I play sport _____ .
6 I finish school _____ .

> **WRITING TIP**
>
> Make it better! ✓ ✓ ✓
> Write some things you <u>don't</u> do and say why.
> _I don't play sport because I don't like it._

8 Write sentences with the words below.

1 play football after school ✗ / don't like it
  I don't play football after school because I don't
  like it.

2 chat online ✗ / haven't got a computer
  _____

3 watch TV in the evening ✗ / it's boring
  _____

4 play video games ✗ / I like chess
  _____

5 go swimming ✗ / it's very cold!
  _____

PLAN

9 Make notes about your typical week. Use Exercises 2 and 5 to help you.

WRITE

10 Write a blog post about your typical week. Look at page 29 of the Student's Book to help you.

_____
_____
_____
_____
_____
_____
_____
_____
_____
_____
_____
_____

CHECK

11 Check your writing. Can you say YES to the questions?

- Are there activities from Exercises 2 and 5 in your blog?
- Are there time expressions to say when you do the activities?
- Are there activities you do not do and do you say why?
- Are the spelling and punctuation correct?

Do you need to write a second draft?

Vocabulary
Daily routines

1 Complete the text with the words in the box. There is one extra word.

> breakfast do dressed make
> shower go to teeth ~~up~~

My daily routine

I get ¹ _up_ at 6.30 am. Then I have a ² _____ and brush my ³ _____ . I get ⁴ _____ in jeans and a T-shirt. Then I have ⁵ _____ with my mum and dad. I ⁶ _____ school at 8.30 am and finish at 3 pm. In the evening, I ⁷ _____ my homework and watch TV.

Total: 6

After school activities

2 Complete the sentences with the words in the box.

> football ~~chess~~ dance drama
> art swimming karate

1 I want to play a game. Let's play ___chess___ .
2 I want to paint pictures. Let's have _____ classes.
3 I want to learn to fight. Let's do _____ .
4 I want to learn the tango. Let's have _____ classes.
5 I want to be an actor. Let's do _____ classes.
6 I want to go to the sea. Let's go _____ .
7 I want to go to the park. Let's play _____ .

Total: 6

Language focus
Present simple: affirmative, negative and questions

3 Complete the sentences with the correct form of the verbs in brackets.

1 We ___study___ English in the afternoon. (study)
2 Jake _____ Art and Music. (not study)
3 Jenny _____ football at school. (play)
4 They _____ near us. (not live)
5 I _____ lunch at home. (have)
6 You _____ to school by bus. (not go)
7 Jane _____ school at 4 pm. (finish)

Total: 6

4 Complete the questions and answers. Use the verbs in brackets.

1 A: ___Do___ you ___study___ Art? (study)
    B: Yes, I ___do___ .
2 A: _____ your sister _____ to school with you? (go)
    B: Yes, she _____ .
3 A: _____ your parents _____ you with your homework? (help)
    B: No, they _____ .
4 A: _____ time _____ your school _____ ? (start)
    B: At 8 am.
5 A: _____ often _____ you _____ sport? (play)
    B: Every day.

Total: 6

5 Complete the questions with a question word from the box and *do* or *does*.

> When Where (x2) Who What ~~What time~~

1 A: ___What time do___ you usually get up?
    B: About 8.00.
2 A: _____ your mum work?
    B: In an office.
3 A: _____ your teacher give the class homework?
    B: On Thursdays.
4 A: _____ you live with?
    B: My mum and dad.
5 A: _____ you do at the weekend?
    B: I do sport.
6 A: _____ your best friend live?
    B: In Moscow.

Total: 5

Adverbs of frequency

6 (Circle) the correct options.

1 I ___ early in the morning.
   (a) usually get up   **b** get up usually

2 I ___ tennis at the weekend.
   a play often   **b** often play

3 I ___ late for school.
   a am never   **b** never am

4 I ___ happy on Saturday morning.
   a always am   **b** am always

5 I ___ lunch with my friends.
   a sometimes have   **b** have sometimes

Total: 4

Language builder

7 Complete the conversation with the missing words. (Circle) the correct options.

> **Debbie:** ¹___ any brothers or sisters?
> **Scott:** Yes, I ²___ . I've got one brother. ³___ brothers and sisters have you got?
> **Debbie:** I ⁴___ any brothers or sisters. How often ⁵___ sport?
> **Scott:** I ⁶___ swimming with my brother after school. What about you?
> **Debbie:** I ⁷___ tennis! ⁸___ to the sports centre?
> **Scott:** Yes, I do. ⁹___ do you play tennis?
> **Debbie:** At the park. ¹⁰___ house is near the park.
> **Scott:** My ¹¹___ house is near the park, too. Let's play tennis together one day.
> **Debbie:** OK!

1 **(a)** Have you got   **b** You have got
2 **a** have   **b** have got
3 **a** How many   **b** Who
4 **a** not have got   **b** haven't got
5 **a** you do   **b** do you do
6 **a** go often   **b** often go
7 **a** loves   **b** love
8 **a** Do go you   **b** Do you go
9 **a** Where   **b** When
10 **a** Our   **b** His
11 **a** uncle   **b** uncle's

Total: 10

Vocabulary builder

8 Circle the correct option.

1 I have **(lunch)** / **exercise** at school with my classmates.
2 They live in Paris. They're **Spanish** / **French**.
3 Steve **plays** / **does** karate on Tuesdays.
4 My eyes are green and my sister's eyes are **straight** / **brown**.
5 I **go to bed** / **get up** at 7 am and have breakfast.
6 We always do **drama** / **tennis** on Mondays.
7 I get dressed before I **go to school** / **have a shower**.
8 Matthew and Elizabeth are my **brothers** / **best friends**.
9 I never play **chess** / **swimming** with my friends.
10 My sister's hair is very **intelligent** / **curly**.

Total: 9

Speaking

9 Put the words in the correct order to make phrases for asking for information.

1 it / much / How / does / cost / ?
   How much does it cost?

2 is / time / What / the class / ?
   _____

3 days / the classes / are / What / ?
   _____

4 about / you / the / know / Do / classes / ?
   _____

Total: 3

Total: 55

Present simple: affirmative, negative and *Yes/No* questions

Remember that:
- with the present simple we use *'s* with *he*, *she* and *it*.
- we use *doesn't*, not ~~*don't*~~, with *he*, *she* and *it*.
- we use *do* or *does* in *Yes/No* and *Wh-* questions.

1 **Find and correct four more mistakes with the present simple.**

Dylan Taylor ~~don't~~ _doesn't_ ∧ get up early for school, he doesn't go to school by bus, and he doesn't wear a school uniform; in fact, he don't go to school at all! So what does he do every day? Well, Dylan is home educated – he study at home and his dad is his teacher! So, what does he study? His dad teach him subjects like Maths and Science, and Dylan studies other subjects on the Internet with a tutor.

'You like school at home, Dylan?'

'It's good and bad: my dad's a great teacher, but I haven't got any classmates – only my little sister, and she's one year old!'

2 **Correct the mistakes in the questions.**

1 What you want to do?
   What do you want to do?

2 Do he have a shower in the morning?
   _____

3 You have dinner at 8 o'clock?
   _____

4 When goes he to bed?
   _____

5 Does he likes music?
   _____

6 What time you do your homework?
   _____

7 Does school starts at 9 o'clock?
   _____

Prepositions of time

Remember that:
- we use *on*, not ~~*in*~~, with days and dates.
  ✓ The dance class is *on Friday / on 31st January*.
  ✗ The dance class is ~~*in Friday / in 31st January*~~.
- we use *at*, not ~~*to*~~, with time.
  ✓ *Come to my house at five o'clock*.
  ✗ *Come to my house ~~to~~ five o'clock*.
- we use *in*, not ~~*on*~~, with periods in a day.
  ✓ *Lily does exercise in the morning*.
  ✗ *Lily does exercise ~~on~~ the morning*.
- we use *at*, not ~~*in*~~, with 'night' and 'the weekend'.
  ✓ *I do my homework at night / at the weekend*.
  ✗ *I do my homework ~~in~~ night / ~~in~~ the weekend*.

3 **Choose the correct prepositions.**

1 The class is **on / at / (in)** the morning.
2 He usually studies **on / at / in** night.
3 It's **on / at / in** Wednesdays and Fridays.
4 The first class is **on / at / in** 15th April.
5 It finishes **on / at / in** 12 o'clock.
6 I don't do homework **on / at / in** the weekend.
7 David goes to school **on / at / in** the afternoon.
8 My birthday is **on / at / in** 2nd March.

Spell it right! Time words

Remember to spell these time words correctly.

hour	~~houer~~	minutes	~~minuts~~
o'clock	~~oclock~~	always	~~allways~~
tomorrow	~~tomorow~~	usually	~~usualy~~
afternoon	~~afternoom~~	weekend	~~week-end~~

4 **Underline and correct the mistake in each sentence.**

1 Paul plays football on Tuesday
   <u>afternoom</u>.   _afternoon_
2 I allways brush my teeth after
   breakfast.   _____
3 I usualy have lunch at school.   _____
4 At the week end I don't do
   homework.   _____
5 I do exercise for two houers every
   night.   _____
6 The barbecue starts at eight oclock.   _____
7 Do you want to go to the park
   tomorow?   _____
8 I've got a class in five minuts.   _____

3 Schooldays

Vocabulary

Places in a school

1 ★ Put the letters in order to make ten places in a school. Write them under the correct picture.

> pssrot lhal   yarbril
> sloscarom   IT romo
> iylgpna lidef
> necsice bla
> niam lhla
> ~~aceennt~~

1 _canteen_

2 _____

3 _____

4 _____

5 _____

6 _____

7 _____

8 _____

2 ★★ Complete the text about Dani's Tuesdays with words from Exercise 1.

On Tuesdays we've got a long day. It starts in the ¹ _main hall_ with everybody together. Then we go to the ² _____ for our English class. At break time I sometimes go to the ³ _____ outside to play football with my friends. After the break we've got study-hour in the ⁴ _____ . I have lunch in the ⁵ _____ – the food is horrible! – but after lunch we go in the ⁶ _____ and chat or play basketball. In the afternoon we've got an ICT lesson in the ⁷ _____ . The day finishes with experiments in the ⁸ _____ – I'm not very good at these, so I'm always happy when I go home and relax!

3 ★★★ Write sentences about your favourite places in your school. When do you go there?

I like the library. I sometimes go there after school and do my homework. It's very big with a lot of books and four or five computers with the Internet.

4 ★★★ Write at least five other places in a school. Use a dictionary if necessary.

5 ★★★ Write at least five sentences about your perfect school.

Language focus 1

can for ability and permission

1 ★ (Circle) the correct words.

Is your school strict?

Alice: Well, yes and no. At break time we ¹(**can**)/ **can't** decide where to go. We ² **can** / **can't** stay in the classroom or go outside to the playing field, but we ³ **can** / **can't** go out to the shops and of course we ⁴ **can** / **can't** go home!

Karl: Yes, the teachers are very strict! We ⁵ **can** / **can't** talk in class and so we ⁶ **can** / **can't** ask questions. We ⁷ **can** / **can't** listen to the teacher and copy from the board. That's all!

Jane: Not really, no. We use laptops in class and we ⁸ **can** / **can't** go on the Internet to look for information, but we ⁹ **can** / **can't** go on social networking sites, of course! We ¹⁰ **can** / **can't** work in groups in class too. I like that.

2 ★★ Write *can* or *can't* and the verbs in brackets.

1 Usain Bolt ___*can run*___ 100 m very quickly, but he ___*can't run*___ a marathon. (run/run)

2 In many states of the USA you _____ a car when you're 16, but you _____ a bus until you're 21. (drive/drive)

3 The red kangaroo is an amazing animal. It _____ at 40 kph and it _____ a distance of 12 m. (travel/jump)

4 We _____ our mobile phones to school, but we _____ them in class. (take/use)

5 Flying fish _____ out of the water and _____ for about 50 m. (jump/fly)

3 ★★★ Write questions with *can* and the correct answers.

1 children / study at home / in your country?
   Can children study at home in your country?
   No, they can't. (✗)

2 I / use my laptop / in the exam?
   _____
   _____ (✓)

3 penguins / fly?
   _____
   _____ (✗)

4 Pep Guardiola / speak four languages?
   _____
   _____ (✓)

5 you / leave school / when you're fifteen?
   _____
   _____ (✗)

6 we / use our skateboards to go to school?
   _____
   _____ (✗)

4 ★★ Put the words in the correct order to make questions. Answer the questions for you.

1 you / speak / Can / Chinese / ?
   Can you speak Chinese?   Yes, I can.

2 you / Can / swim / ?
   _____

3 talk / in / your / to / Can / you / friends / class / ?
   _____

4 you / do / Can / karate / ?
   _____

5 friends / play / chess / your / Can / ?
   _____

6 your / tennis / parents / play / Can / ?
   _____

Explore nouns and verbs

5 ★★ (Circle) the correct words.

1 I like swimming. It's good (exercise)/ exercising .

2 I go to **training** / **train** on Wednesdays.

3 We have football **practice** / **practise** tomorrow.

4 Be careful here, please! No **run** / **running** !

5 When my **study** / **studies** are over, I want to get a job.

Listening and vocabulary

School subjects

1 ★★ **Use the clues to complete the crossword.**

across

1 People speak this language in France.
4 In this subject you sing or play instruments.
8 You learn about countries and the physical world in this subject.
9 You do this in the sports hall or on the playing field.

down

2 This is about important events in the past.
3 You learn about computers in this subject.
5 You learn about Physics, Chemistry and Biology in this subject.
6 You practise this subject in this book.
7 This subject is about numbers.

Listening

2 ★★ 🔊 **05 Listen to an interview about home education. Tick (✓) the things in the list that Rachel does.**

a She studies with a home tutor. ☐
b She does projects. ☐
c She watches documentaries. ☐
d She goes to museums. ☐
e She wears a uniform. ☐
f She does science experiments. ☐

3 ★★★ 🔊 **05 Listen again and answer the questions.**

1 Who does Rachel organise her work with?
   Her mum.
2 Where can she find information for projects?

3 Where can she visit museums?

4 Where does she go with other home-educated children?

5 What are her favourite subjects?

6 Why can't she do experiments at home?

Language focus 2

(don't) like, don't mind, love, hate + ing

1 ★ **Put the verbs in the correct box.**

hate   love   like   don't like   don't mind

☺☺☺	☺	☺	☹	☹☹☹

2 ★ (Circle) **the correct words in the grammar table.**

1	I love **listen / listening** to music.
2	She hates **start / starting** school at 8.00.

3 ★★ **Write sentences with the prompts.**

1 I / not like / do / homework at the weekend
   I don't like doing homework at the weekend.

2 He / love / play / football / friends
   _____

3 We / hate / watch / documentaries
   _____

4 Isabel / like / have / art classes
   _____

5 Peter / not mind / play / chess
   _____

Object pronouns

4 ★★ **Write the correct object pronoun under each picture.**

① he – _____*him*_____   ② it – _____

③ they – _____   ④ you – _____

⑤ I – _____   ⑥ we – _____

⑦ she – _____

like, love, don't mind, hate + object pronoun

5 ★★★ **Answer the questions with *like*, *love*, *don't mind*, *hate* and an object pronoun.**

1 Are you a fan of Justin Bieber?
   Yes, I like him.
   _____

2 Do you like learning English?
   _____

3 Do you like the singer Taylor Swift?
   _____

4 Are you interested in History?
   _____

5 Do you like cats?
   _____

6 Are you a fan of Taylor Lautner from *Twilight*?
   _____

Explore adjectives

6 ★★ **Try to improve your writing by using sentences with adjectives. Complete the blog with the sentences in the box.**

I̶t̶'̶s̶ ̶g̶r̶e̶a̶t̶.̶   It's an interesting subject.
He's brilliant!   It's really boring!
I'm a really fast swimmer.   He's really slow!

> Everyone likes the school. ¹ _It's great._
> At my school we study different subjects. I love Science. ² _____
> But I hate Maths. ³ _____ But my favourite subject is History because of our teacher, Mr Langley. ⁴ _____
> We do lots of sports. I like swimming. ⁵ _____ I also play football with my friend Freddy. He's not a very good player. ⁶ _____ But we have fun.

7 ★★★ **Complete the sentences with your own ideas. Then tell your partner.**

1 I think _____ is an interesting subject.
2 I'm a really fast _____ .
3 I think _____ is really boring.
4 My friend _____ is a brilliant _____ .
5 _____ is great. I love it!

Reading

1 ★ **Read about Eton College. Which of these things is not in the text?**

1 the history of the school
2 a student's daily routine
3 famous people from the school
4 the cost of the school
5 the school facilities
6 where the boys live

Eton College

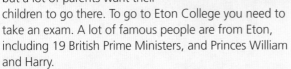

In England a 'public school' is a private independent school. One famous public school is Eton College, opened by King Henry VI in 1440. The school and the uniforms are very old.

Eton is a *boarding school* for 1,290 boys aged from 13 to 18. It costs £30,000 a year, but a lot of parents want their children to go there. To go to Eton College you need to take an exam. A lot of famous people are from Eton, including 19 British Prime Ministers, and Princes William and Harry.

Boys have got a simple study-bedroom and join a 'house' of 50 students. They've got 35 classes (called 'divs' by the boys) a week, with 10 or 20 students, and they also *discuss* their work with personal *tutors*. There are 160 teachers, or 'beaks'.

Eton is a very big school with amazing *facilities*. It has got nine libraries, three theatres, an Olympic *rowing* lake and a lot of football and rugby *pitches*. It has got an art building, 24 Science labs, and even a Natural History Museum!

2 ★★ **Match the words in *bold italics* in the text with the definitions.**

1 These teachers work with one student. _____
2 You play rugby or football on these. _____
3 To talk about something. _____
4 A school where students sleep, eat and go to class. _____
5 A sport where you sit in a boat and move it with your arms. _____
6 Places where you can do special activities. _____

3 ★★ **Match the numbers in the text with the meanings.**

1 1440
2 1,290
3 £30,000
4 19
5 9
6 160

a the number of libraries at Eton
b the number of British Prime Ministers from Eton
c the year when Eton started
d the cost of the school for a student for one year
e the number of teachers at Eton
f the number of students in the school

4 ★★★ **Are these boys students at Eton? Tick (✓) Yes or No.**

	Yes	No
1 'I don't wear a uniform in my school.'		
2 'Hurry up! The beak's coming!'		
3 'My name's Sebastian and I'm 11 years old.'		
4 'My tutor's name is Mr Harris.'		
5 'There are 50 boys in my house.'		
6 'My school has only got one Science lab.'		

5 ★★★ **What do you think is good about Eton? What don't you like? Write your ideas about the text.**

> **READING TIP**
> To find specific information in a text, scan it – read it quickly with your finger under the words to help you – to find the information you need.

Writing

An email

1 Read Simon's email. Where does he spend a lot of time?

To: Liam
Subject: Seven Oaks Academy

Hey Liam

How are you doing? My new school (Seven Oaks Academy) is amazing! My class is small so the teachers have time to help everyone. We decide the subjects we want to study in class, and we can work on projects together in groups.

We've got an IT room so we can find the information we need (we don't use course books), and we can use tablets in class – but I haven't got one. ☹ You know I love Science so I spend a lot of time in the science lab. This school's really different from the old one. I love it!

How are things at your new school?

Cheers

Simon

2 Read the email again. Mark the sentences true (*T*) or false (*F*).

1 Simon likes his new school.   _T_
2 There are a lot of students in his class.   ___
3 He doesn't study any subjects.   ___
4 Simon has got a lot of books.   ___
5 Liam is at a new school.   ___

3 Look back at Simon's email. What informal language does he use?

1 an abbreviation: _lab_
2 to start the email: _____
3 to end the email: _____
4 contractions: _____

4 Complete the email with the words in the box.

> It's   asap   Bye   's   Hey   've

To: Jane
Subject: School

¹_____ Jane

How are you? Here ²_____ a photo of me with my new friends from school. ³_____ great here. They ⁴_____ got big classrooms and the teachers are friendly so I'm happy.

What's your new school like? Write to me ⁵_____ !

⁶_____ for now.

Laura

Writing

5 **Join the sentences with *so*.**

1 I love playing football. I spend a lot of time outside.

_____

2 The school is small. There aren't many teachers.

_____

3 I've got a tablet. I can find information in class.

_____

4 We've got a school uniform. We can't wear jeans.

_____

5 The school isn't near my house. I take the bus.

_____

6 **Match the questions with the answers.**

1 What's the name of the school?
2 Are the teachers nice?
3 What subjects do you study?
4 How do you study?
5 What facilities has it got?
6 Are the classrooms good?

a Yes, they are. They're big and old with posters on the walls.
b We don't use course books and we work in groups.
c Forest High.
d They are very friendly.
e It's got a theatre and a swimming pool.
f Maths, English and we can study three languages.

7 **Read Simon's email again. Find examples of addressing the reader.**

8 **Which of these sentences does <u>not</u> address the reader?**

1 How are you doing?
2 As you know, I'm not good at Maths.
3 The teachers are all very nice.
4 Thanks for your email.
5 Do you like your new school?

9 **Read Simon's email again. Tick (✓) the things he writes about.**

the name of the school ☐
the teachers ☐
the subjects you can take ☐
the classrooms ☐
course books ☐
other students ☐
the uniform ☐
the timetable ☐

PLAN

10 **Imagine you are at a new school. Look at the topics in Exercise 9 and make notes. Include some good things and some bad things.**

WRITE

11 **Write an email to Simon about your new school. Look at page 41 of the Student's Book to help you.**

_____
_____
_____
_____
_____
_____
_____
_____
_____
_____
_____
_____
_____

CHECK

12 **Check your writing. Can you say YES to the questions?**

• Are the topics from Exercise 9 in your email?
• Are there questions and sentences addressing the reader?
• Are there good things and bad things?
• Are the spelling and punctuation correct?

Do you need to write a second draft?

3 Review

Vocabulary
Places in a school

1 Circle the correct words.
1 We have lunch in the science lab / canteen.
2 We study ICT in the IT room / main hall.
3 You can read lots of books in the playing field / library.
4 We play football on the playing field / in the IT room.
5 The headteacher sometimes talks to everyone in the main hall / library.
6 We have PE in the sports hall / library.
7 We learn about how the world works in the sports hall / science lab.
8 We spend most of the school day in the library / classroom.

Total: 7

School subjects

2 Write the names of the school subjects.
1 computers   ICT
2 guitar   _____
3 *Bonjour!*   _____
4 cities and countries _____
5 8 x 14   _____
6 Time to do an experiment! _____
7 World War 1   _____
8 Do some exercise. _____
9 Listen and repeat. _____

Total: 8

Language focus
can for ability and permission

3 Look at the information in the table. Complete the sentences and questions.

	swim	speak French	ride a bike	play the guitar
Kristin	✓	✗	✓	✓
Leo	✗	✗	✓	✗

1 Kristin _____can_____ swim.
2 Leo _____ swim.
3 Kristin and Leo _____ a bike.
4 A: _____ (Kristin) the guitar?
  B: Yes, _____ .
5 A: _____ (Leo) French?
  B: No, _____ .
6 A: _____ (Kristin and Leo) speak French?
  B: No, _____ .

Total: 8

Object pronouns

4 Complete the sentences with the correct object pronoun from the box.

me   us   him   it   her   you   them

1 I can't eat this food. Do you want _____it_____ ?
2 Ruth is late. Can you call _____ ?
3 We can't speak English. Can you help _____ ?
4 I don't like bananas. Do you like _____ ?
5 Where is the main hall? Can you tell _____ ?
6 She doesn't want to talk to me, she wants to talk to _____ .
7 Mark plays tennis every weekend. Do you want to play with _____ ?

Total: 6

(don't) like, don't mind, love, hate + ing

5 Complete the sentences using the key and the correct form of the verbs in brackets.

> love ☺☺☺   like ☺   don't mind ☺
> don't like ☹   hate ☹☹☹

1 I *like playing football* . (☺ / play football)
2 He _____ . (☹ / study Maths)
3 We _____ . (☺ / do homework)
4 They _____ . (☺☺☺ / listen to music)
5 She _____ . (☹☹☹ / be late for school)
6 I _____ . (☺ / watch films)

Total: 5

Vocabulary builder

6 Circle the correct options.

1 I use my ___ to listen to music.
  a guitar   **b** MP3 player   **c** console
2 I'm from Brazil. I speak ___ .
  a Portugal   **b** Portuguese   **c** Portugalese
3 Your mother's brother is your ___ .
  a cousin   **b** aunt   **c** uncle
4 My favourite colours are green and ___ .
  a curly   **b** long   **c** brown
5 I usually have ___ before I go to school.
  a dinner   **b** lunch   **c** breakfast
6 I always ___ my homework in the evening.
  a do   **b** make   **c** have
7 I ___ late on Saturdays – at 10 am.
  a go to bed   **b** get up   **c** have lunch
8 We do ___ at school on Fridays.
  a karate   **b** chess   **c** tennis
9 Her hair is ___ .
  a tall   **b** spiky   **c** small
10 My favourite sport is ___ .
  a music   **b** drama   **c** football

Total: 9

Language builder

7 Complete the conversation with the missing words. Circle the correct options.

> **Vicky:** [1]___ Science?
> **Lisa:** I love [2]___ !
> **Vicky:** [3]___ your teacher give you a lot of homework?
> **Lisa:** Yes, but I like [4]___ . [5]___ subject do you like best?
> **Vicky:** I like ICT. [6]___ got new computers in our school.
> **Lisa:** [7]___ use them to play games?
> **Vicky:** No, we [8]___ . How about you?
> **Lisa:** I can play games on my computer at home. I use my [9]___ game console when he's out. [10]___ got some new computer games. Do you want to come over and play [11]___ ?
> **Vicky:** Yes, please! [12]___ do you live?

1 **a** Do you like   **b** You do like   **c** You are like
2 **a** it   **b** him   **c** them
3 **a** Can   **b** Do   **c** Does
4 **a** it   **b** them   **c** they
5 **a** Where   **b** What   **c** When
6 **a** We do   **b** We're   **c** We've
7 **a** You can   **b** Can you   **c** Do you can
8 **a** don't   **b** aren't   **c** can't
9 **a** brother   **b** brother's   **c** brothers
10 **a** He's   **b** He does   **c** He is
11 **a** it   **b** them   **c** they
12 **a** Where   **b** What   **c** When

Total: 11

Speaking

8 Put the sentences in the correct order to make the conversation.

___ **A:** OK, can I go tomorrow night?
_1_ **A:** Hi, Mum. Can I go to Dana's house tonight?
___ **A:** Great, thanks Mum!
___ **A:** Why not?
___ **B:** Yes, you can.
___ **B:** Because your grandmother's here tonight.
___ **B:** No, sorry, I'm afraid you can't, Sandra.

Total: 6

Total: 60

can for ability and permission

> Remember, we use the infinitive without *to* after *can/can't*.
>
> ✓ He *can* speak three languages.
> ✗ He can ~~to speak~~ three languages.
> ✗ He can ~~speaking~~ three languages.
> ✗ He can ~~speaks~~ three languages.

1 Find and correct five more mistakes with can.

Tim:	Hi, Daniel, I want to paint my bedroom on Saturday. Can you ~~helping~~ *help* ˄me?
Daniel:	No, I can't help you on Saturday, I've got football practice. :-(
Tim:	Can you to come on Sunday?
Daniel:	Yes, I can visiting you in the afternoon. Is that OK?
Tim:	Brilliant! Thanks! Can you to start at 2 o'clock?
Daniel:	Yes, that's OK. I can meet you at the paint shop at 2 o'clock.
Tim:	OK. We can to buy some snacks, too.
Daniel:	I haven't got any old clothes for painting. Can you giving me some?
Tim:	Of course I can!
Daniel:	Brilliant! See you on Sunday! :-)

like, love, hate, don't mind + object pronoun

> Remember:
> * we use an object pronoun after *like, love, hate, don't mind*
> ✓ I study French. I really like *it*.
> ✗ I study French. I really ~~like~~.
> * we use *him* for boys and men, and *her* for girls and women
> ✓ That's John's sister. I really like *her*.
> ✗ That's John's sister. I really like ~~him~~.
> * for animals and things, we use *it* (singular) and *them* (plural)

2 Read the conversation. Find and correct four more mistakes.

Jack:	This is a photo of people at my school. Do you know them?
Emily:	No. Who is that? Is she your teacher?
Jack:	Yes, that's Mrs Miller. I really like ~~him~~ ˄ *her*. She teaches English.
Emily:	Do you like English?
Jack:	Yes, I love! What about you?
Emily:	I don't mind it. What about French? Do you study that?
Jack:	Yeah but I hate it.
Emily:	Who's your French teacher?
Jack:	That's him. I don't like. He's very strict!
Emily:	Do you like the people in your class?
Jack:	Oh, yes. I love. They're brilliant! We have great fun.
Emily:	And who is this girl?
Jack:	Ah, that's Maria. She's beautiful. I really like him …

Spell it right! Adjectives

> Remember to spell these adjectives from the unit correctly:
>
> | | | |
> |---|---|---|
> | ~~diffrent~~ | ~~diferent~~ | different |
> | ~~favourit~~ | ~~favorit~~ | favourite |
> | ~~famouse~~ | ~~famus~~ | famous |
> | ~~greate~~ | ~~grate~~ | great |
> | ~~importent~~ | ~~importan~~ | important |
> | ~~intresting~~ | ~~intersting~~ | interesting |

3 Underline and correct the mistake in each sentence.

1 At my school we study <u>diffrent</u> subjects.
   different
2 I think Geography is an intresting subject.
   _____
3 History is about important events in the past.
   _____
4 Football is greate. I love it!
   _____
5 What are your favorit subjects?
   _____
6 A lot of famouse people are from Eton.
   _____

Vocabulary

Food

1 ★ **Find the words for food in the wordsquare.**

f	r	b	a	n	a	n	a	s	c	u	t
c	i	a	p	p	l	e	s	e	q	l	h
a	k	l	h	r	j	p	b	g	a	s	r
r	e	m	x	g	e	y	r	r	i	m	e
r	c	t	i	y	i	t	e	f	s	e	t
o	e	l	b	l	r	p	a	s	s	a	t
t	r	e	s	g	k	k	d	w	g	t	u
s	h	n	h	c	o	t	i	m	g	d	b
c	h	i	c	k	e	n	x	t	e	o	t
a	c	s	l	c	v	h	p	j	k	e	g
g	k	p	i	t	a	t	h	e	s	s	e

2 ★★ **Complete the text about Jo's food habits with the words in the box.**

> pasta   rice   cheese   carrots   ~~milk~~
> meat   pizza   beans   bread

What do teenagers in the UK like to eat? What do we hate? I think I'm typical. I don't eat breakfast because I don't have time. I just drink a glass of [1] _____*milk*_____. Then, I usually eat a [2] _____ sandwich at break time because I can't wait until lunch! I eat a lot of white [3] _____. My mum says this is unhealthy. I love Italian food, and for lunch at school I often have [4] _____ or [5] _____. I don't really like vegetables but I sometimes eat [6] _____. I like their orange colour!
My favourite meal is chilli con carne. I cook this with my dad. You just need [7] _____, [8] _____ and [9] _____. It's really good!

3 ★★★ **Read the clues and write the names of the food.**

1 These are long, straight orange vegetables.
   c _*arrots*_____

2 They're yellow and monkeys like them.
   b _____

3 They come from chickens.
   e _____

4 Use a knife to put this on bread.
   b _____

5 It's white and you drink it.
   m _____

6 They live in the sea and we eat them.
   f _____

7 They are long, green vegetables. Cook them in water.
   b _____

8 It's white. Cook it in hot water.
   r _____

Language focus 1

Countable and uncountable nouns

1 ★ ⟨Circle⟩ the correct words in the grammar table.

1	Countable / Uncountable nouns can be singular and plural.
2	Countable / Uncountable nouns have no plural.
3	We use *a/an* with **a singular countable / an uncountable** noun.
4	We use *some* with **affirmative / negative** plural and uncountable nouns.
5	We use *any* with **affirmative / negative** plural and uncountable nouns.

2 ★★ ⟨Circle⟩ the correct food words.
1 I've got a ⟨banana⟩ / carrots in my bag.
2 Have we got any banana / cheese?
3 Joe's got an milk / egg for breakfast.
4 We haven't got any bread / apple.
5 They've got some carrot / meat, but they haven't got any rice / vegetable.
6 We've got some oranges / apple.

a/an, some and any

3 ★★ Complete the text with *a/an*, *some* or *any*.

Andres Ramos is a footballer. He loves meat, but he doesn't eat a lot these days, and he doesn't eat ¹ ___any___ takeaway food. Here's what he's got to eat today:
Breakfast: ² _____ fruit, ³ _____ big plate of eggs and ⁴ _____ bread. ⁵ _____ milk.
Snack after training: ⁶ _____ energy drink and ⁷ _____ bananas.
Lunch: ⁸ _____ fish, a lot of potatoes and ⁹ _____ vegetables. ¹⁰ _____ water.
Dinner: ¹¹ _____ burger and chips and ¹² _____ ice cream – it's his birthday!
Andres is a professional, so he doesn't eat ¹³ _____ chocolate or biscuits or drink ¹⁴ _____ fizzy drinks, but he loves them!

🔍 Explore expressions with *have* 2

4 ★★ Complete the sentences with one of the words from the box.

> lunch   problem   ~~fun~~   snack   breakfast   party

1 I always have ___*fun*___ at my sister's house because there's lots to do there.
2 My brother wants to cook dinner for my parents tonight but he has a _____ . He can't cook!
3 Can I have a _____ for my birthday next month?
4 I know dinner is at 6 o'clock but I'm hungry now. Can I have a _____ ?
5 We have _____ at 7.00 every morning. We have eggs or toast.
6 I usually have _____ at school. I eat fish or meat with rice.

5 ★★★ What food have you got at home? What haven't you got? Write six sentences about things from the list.

> vegetables   fruit   pasta   beans   milk
> carrots   bread   pizza   water   eggs

We've got some milk in the fridge. I've got some water in my room.

6 ★★★ Plan your menu for tomorrow. Use Exercise 3 as an example. What do you eat for each meal? Use a dictionary if necessary.

Breakfast: an egg, some bread and some orange juice.

Listening and vocabulary

Meals

1 ★ **Put the dishes in the correct place in the table.**

chocolate cake

burger and chips

soup

ice cream

roast chicken

salad

bananas

chocolate bar

starter	main course	dessert	snack
salad			

2 ★★ **Match the food on page 37 with the words below.**

breakfast   lunch   dinner

breakfast – eggs

Listening

3 ★ 🔊 06 **Listen to the conversation. Match the pictures (1–3) with the speakers.**

Charlie   Helen   Simon

①

②

③

4 ★★★ 🔊 06 **Listen again. Complete the table with the correct food and drink.**

Charlie	Simon	Helen

5 ★★★ **Answer the questions.**
1 Who's hungry?   *Charlie*
2 Who wants a bit of chocolate?   _____
3 Who tries the bean salad?   _____
4 Who had a party yesterday?   _____
5 Who wants some cake?   _____
6 What doesn't Simon want in the end?

_____

Language focus 2

there is / there are

1 ★ Circle the correct words in the grammar table.

1	*There is a* + **singular / plural** countable noun.
2	*There is some* + **countable / uncountable** noun.
3	*There are some* + **singular / plural** countable noun.
4	*There isn't/aren't* **some / any** + noun.

2 ★★ Complete the sentences. Use *is* or *are* and *a/an* or *some*.

Fridge A

There ¹ *is an*_____ egg.

There ² _____ cola.

There ³ _____ bananas.

There ⁴ _____ olives.

There ⁵ _____ carrot.

Fridge B

There ⁶ _____ milk.

There ⁷ _____ tomatoes.

There ⁸ _____ cheese.

There ⁹ _____ bottle of water.

There ¹⁰ _____ orange.

3 ★★ Correct the incorrect sentences.

    is

1 There ~~are~~ some cheese in the fridge.

2 Is there any milk?

3 There aren't an apples.

4 There are any bananas?

5 Is there any rice?

6 There aren't any pasta.

much / many / a lot of

4 ★ Circle the correct options. Then do the quiz.

① How **much** / **many** water is there in a carrot?
 a 66% **b** 84% **c** 91%

② How **much** / **many** pizzas do Americans eat in a year?
 a 1 billion **b** 3 billion **c** 5 billion

③ How **much** / **many** calories are there in an orange?
 a 50 **b** 65 **c** 30

④ How **much** / **many** milk is there in 1 kilo of cheese?
 a 10 litres **b** 5 litres **c** 3 litres

⑤ True or false? There are **much** / **a lot of** calories in 100 grams of chocolate.
 a True, about 520. **b** False, about 120.

Explore international words

5 ★★ Match the international words with the definitions.

tacos	~~burger~~	pizza	sushi	curry	lasagne

1 A lot of people think they're from Germany but they're American. *burger*

2 This delicious food is from Naples in Italy. _____

3 It's usually fish and rice and it's Japanese. _____

4 It's a traditional dish from Mexico, with chicken, meat or cheese. _____

5 This is a dish from Italy with pasta and meat. _____

6 This food is from India but it's very popular in the UK. _____

Reading

1 ★ **Read the text about pizzas. Tick (✓) the cities and countries in the text.**

New York	☐	Tokyo	☐	Naples	☐
the UK	☐	Japan	☐	the USA	☐
Milan	☐	Italy	☐	Colombia	☐

2 ★★ **Complete the definitions with the words in *bold italics* from the text.**

1 A _____ is a kind of sea animal.
2 Pieces of pizza, cake or bread are _____ .
3 _____ are small plants that you put in food and you can eat.
4 If I need _____ two things, I need two things or more.
5 We say there are many _____ of pizzas when there are many different pizzas.
6 A _____ is food on a pizza.

3 ★★ **Read the text again and answer the questions.**

1 How old is pizza in Naples?
   At least 200 years old.
2 What is the topping of a Margherita pizza?
   _____
3 What colour is the Italian flag?
   _____
4 Where is the first pizzeria in the USA?
   _____
5 How many pizzerias are there in the USA now?
   _____
6 How many Americans *don't* eat pizza regularly?
   _____
7 How many slices of pizza do people in the USA eat every second?
   _____
8 What is a popular pizza topping in Colombia?
   _____

4 ★★★ **Read the information in the text again. Are these sentences true (*T*) or false (*F*)?**

1 We know where pizzas come from.   *T*
2 The Margherita pizza has tomato, meat and herbs on it.   ___
3 Lombardi's pizzeria is in New York.   ___
4 Americans like pizzas and they eat a lot of it.   ___
5 People in different countries like different kinds of pizzas.   ___

5 ★★★ **Why is pizza popular? Find ideas in the text and write your own ideas.**

> **READING TIP**
>
> You do not need to understand every word in a text. It is more important to understand the main message in the reading.

What do you know ABOUT PIZZA?

Home	About	News	Reviews

Pizza is a delicious food you can eat all over the world. Here are some pizza facts.

- Pizza comes from Naples in southern Italy and is *at least* 200 years old. The Margherita pizza, with a *topping* of tomato, mozzarella cheese and *herbs*, is red, white and green – the same colours as the Italian flag!
- The first pizzeria in the United States, Lombardi's in Manhattan, New York, is 110 years old. Now there are 61,269 pizzerias in the USA.
- Pizza is a very popular takeaway food in the USA. 94% of Americans eat pizza regularly – and they buy three billion pizzas every year! That's 350 *slices* of pizza every second!
- A popular pizza topping in Japan is *squid* and a popular topping in Colombia is avocado.
- A lot of men like meat toppings and women eat more vegetables. Chicken is the most popular meat topping for a pizza.
- There are a lot of *varieties*, so you can always find a topping you like. What's *your* favourite?

Writing

A report about a special event

1 Read the report about a special event in Greece and look at the pictures. Where do the family go for a picnic?

◄ ►   A traditional celebration   ✕

'Clean Monday' (*Kathari Deftera*) is eight weeks before Easter in February.

A In my family, we start the day preparing the food in the morning.

B We finish our pudding and before we leave the beach, we clean up and my brother and I fly kites.

C It celebrates the first day of spring. It's a public holiday in Greece. Food is very important.

D After that, we have *halva* for pudding.

E All my friends come to the dance too. *Kathari Deftera* is a great tradition! We love it!

F Then we go to the beach with the food for a picnic.

G Then, in the evening we go to the town square for traditional music and dancing.

H The picnic at the beach contains all the traditional food. On 'Clean Monday' we don't eat meat. We eat a special kind of bread, called *lagana*, with seafood dishes, salads and olives.

Kostas Dimitriadis

---

2 Put the sentences in the report in the correct order.

1 _C_   2 ___   3 ___   4 ___
5 ___   6 ___   7 ___   8 ___

Useful language Time connectors _____

3 Read the report again. Complete the time connectors.

1 _____ the morning
2 _____ we leave the beach
3 the first day _____ spring
4 _____ that
5 _____ we go to the beach
6 Then, _____ the evening
7 _____ 'Clean Monday'

4 Complete the text with the time connectors in the box. Sometimes there is more than one possible answer.

> Then   After that   in the morning   On
> After lunch   Before   In the evening

¹_____ my birthday I always get up early. My mum and dad and I have a big breakfast – some orange juice, eggs and toast. ²_____, I go and open my birthday presents. ³_____ I get dressed, I play with my new presents.

We always go to my grandparents' house ⁴_____. ⁵_____ we go out for lunch. I always have chicken and chips – my favourite food! ⁶_____, we have a birthday cake at home. I love it!

⁷_____, we usually watch a film together or play video games.

Writing

> **WRITING TIP**
>
> Make it better! ✓ ✓ ✓
> Time phrases can go at the beginning or at the
> end of a sentence.
> *In the evening* I play tennis.
> I play tennis *in the evening*.

5 **Answer the questions. Use full sentences.**

1 What do you do in the morning?
In the morning I go to school.

2 What do you do before you go to school?

3 What do you do in the evening?

4 What do you do after you have dinner? And after that?

5 What do you always do before you go to bed?

> **WRITING TIP**
>
> Make it better! ✓ ✓ ✓
> Use capital letters for cities, countries,
> nationalities, languages, days of the week,
> months and celebrations.
> *London, Argentina, Brazilian, Turkish, Thursday,
> July, New Year's Eve*

6 **Rewrite the sentences with capital letters.**

1 this restaurant has italian pizzas, japanese sushi and mexican tacos.

2 in england, we speak english but a lot of people speak welsh in wales.

3 on monday my mum and dad are going to london to the british museum.

4 in december we go skiing in switzerland.

> **WRITING TIP**
>
> Make it better! ✓ ✓ ✓
> When you use words from a different language,
> say what they mean.
> *In Mexico we eat* **quesadillas**. *They're a delicious
> food with cheese and meat or vegetables.*

7 **Write about things in your country.**

1 Name three dishes and explain them.
*In Spain we eat tortilla. It's a kind of omelette
with eggs and potatoes.*

2 Name two special days and explain them.

8 **Read the article again. Make notes about the things Kostas writes about.**

name of the celebration	Clean Monday
when it is	
what it celebrates	
where they celebrate	
food	
people	
activities	

PLAN

9 **Choose a celebration from a different country to write about. Look for information on the Internet. Make notes for each heading in Exercise 8.**

WRITE

10 **Write a magazine article about the celebration. Look at page 51 of the Student's Book to help you.**

CHECK

11 **Check your writing. Can you say YES to the questions?**

- Are the topics from Exercise 8 in your article?
- Are there time connectors?
- Are the capital letters correct?
- Are there words from another language? Do you explain them?
- Are the spelling and punctuation correct?

Do you need to write a second draft?

Vocabulary
Food

1 **What colour are they? Complete the sentences with the words in the box.**

> bananas ~~bread~~ carrots eggs
> milk cheese apples

1 ____Bread____ is white or brown.
2 _____ are orange.
3 _____ is white.
4 _____ are yellow.
5 _____ are red or green.
6 _____ is yellow.
7 _____ are white or brown.

Total: 6

Meals and courses

2 **Complete the sentences with the words in the box.**

> dessert dinner snack lunch ~~breakfast~~
> starter main course

1 For ____breakfast____ in the morning, I have an egg.
2 Our _____ today is chicken soup.
3 I like ice cream or cake for _____ .
4 My dad usually has _____ at the office.
5 For the _____ we're having fish and chips.
6 In the evening, I do my homework, have _____ and go to bed.
7 We eat a _____ in the playground at 11.00.

Total: 6

Language focus
Countable and uncountable nouns

3 **Find 12 more food and drink words in the wordsnake. Are they countable or uncountable?**

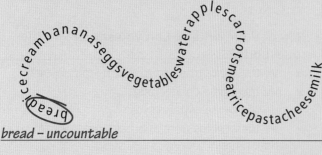

____bread – uncountable____
_____
_____
_____

Total: 24

there is / there are; much / many / a lot of

4 **Complete the conversation with the words in the box.**

> there is many are there a lot of much
> any ~~Are there any~~ there are How many

Alex: Let's make a salad.
Gina: Good idea! ¹ ____Are there any____ vegetables?
Alex: Yes, ² _____ . We've got three carrots.
Gina: ³ _____ tomatoes ⁴ _____ ?
Alex: There aren't ⁵ _____ – just two. But they're quite big.
Gina: How ⁶ _____ cheese is there?
Alex: There's ⁷ _____ cheese.
Gina: Is there ⁸ _____ yoghurt?
Alex: Yes, ⁹ _____ a lot of yoghurt too!

Total: 8

A/an/some/any

5 **Complete the sentences with *a/an/some* or *any*.**

1 I don't like ____any____ vegetables. They're all horrible.

2 Jenny's got _____ sandwich for lunch today.

3 I need to buy _____ milk for my dad.

4 We haven't got _____ carrots. Can you buy _____ tomorrow?

5 Do you eat _____ banana for breakfast every day?

6 There's _____ apple on your desk. Is it yours?

7 You can have _____ ice cream for dessert today.

8 Can I have _____ water please? I'm thirsty.

Total: 8

Vocabulary builder

6 **Circle the correct options.**

1 I eat lunch in the school ___ .
   a library   b lab   **c** canteen

2 We play volleyball in the ___ .
   a main hall   b science lab   c sports hall

3 We learn about other countries in ___ .
   a Science   b Geography   c Art

4 We learn about grammar in ___ .
   a History   b Maths   c French

5 Oranges and apples are two kinds of ___ .
   a fruit   b vegetables   c drinks

6 ___ are red or green.
   a Carrots   b Apples   c Bananas

7 Biscuits and crisps are two kinds of ___ .
   a sandwich   b snack   c breakfast

8 Juice and water are two kinds of ___ .
   a drink   b snack   c lunch

Total: 7

Language builder

7 **Complete the conversation with the missing words. Circle the correct options.**

Ann: What ¹___ in your lunch box today?
Matt: I've got two apples and ²___ cheese sandwich.
Ann: Have you got ³___ vegetables?
Matt: No, I don't like ⁴___ !
Ann: ⁵___ do you usually drink?
Matt: Mum usually gives me ⁶___ fruit juice. My sister ⁷___ juice so Mum gives ⁸___ chocolate milk.
Ann: I see. ⁹___ a good canteen at your school?
Matt: It's OK, but ¹⁰___ many choices. ¹¹___ a good café near the school and we sometimes go there after school.

1 **a** have you got   b you have got   c have got you
2 a some   b a   c an
3 a any   b much   c a
4 a him   b them   c it
5 a Where   b What   c When
6 a some   b any   c much
7 a not like   b don't like   c doesn't like
8 a her   b him   c them
9 a Are there   b Is there   c There are
10 a there isn't   b there aren't   c there haven't
11 a There is   b There are   c There has

Total: 10

Speaking

8 **Complete the conversation with phrases a–d.**

a No, thanks.
b I'd like cheese and tomato, please.
c €2.50, please.
d Can I have a sandwich, please?

Server: What can I get you?
Lucy: ¹_____
Server: Which one would you like?
Lucy: ²_____
Server: Anything else?
Lucy: ³_____
   How much is that?
Server: ⁴_____

Total: 4

Total: 73

much / many / a lot of

Remember that:

- we use **many** in negative sentences with plural countable nouns
  *there aren't ~~much~~ apples ➜ there aren't **many** apples*
- we use **much** in negative sentences with uncountable nouns
  *there isn't ~~many~~ milk ➜ there isn't **much** milk*
- in affirmative sentences we use **a lot of** with plural countable nouns and uncountable nouns
  *there are ~~many~~ bananas ➜ there are **a lot of** bananas*

1 Find and correct five more mistakes in the conversation.

Tom:	How much food have we got for Dad's party, Jane?
Jane:	Well, we've got ~~much~~ ˄ *a lot of* fruit and vegetables, but we haven't got much carrots.
Tom:	That's OK. Dad doesn't like carrots. How much orange juice have we got?
Jane:	Oh no! We haven't got many orange juice!
Tom:	It's OK, we've got a lot fizzy drinks and some milk.
Jane:	OK. But we haven't got many eggs and there isn't many cheese.
Tom:	Don't worry. We can make sandwiches. How much bread is there?
Jane:	Oh, Tom. We haven't got much bread!
Tom:	How many potatoes have we got?
Jane:	Oh, we've got many potatoes.
Tom:	Great! We can have chips! I love chips!
Jane:	Oh, Tom!

there is / there are

Remember that:

- we use **there + is/isn't** with singular countable nouns and uncountable nouns
  *there ~~are~~ a lot of milk ➜ **there is** a lot of milk*
- we use **there + are/aren't** in sentences with plural countable nouns
  *there ~~is~~ a lot of potatoes ➜ **there are** a lot of potatoes*

2 Are the sentences correct? Correct the incorrect sentences.

1 There is a lot of people at the party.
   There are a lot of people at the party.

2 There are some ice cream in the fridge.
   _____

3 Are there a lot of cheese on the pizza?
   _____

4 There are some good restaurants in this town.
   _____

5 Is there a lot of eggs in the salad?
   _____

6 There aren't much orange juice.
   _____

7 There are some milk but there isn't any rice.
   _____

Spell it right! Meals

Remember that:

- we don't usually use *a* or *the* when we talk about meals in a general way
  ✓ *Last night we had dinner in a pizzeria.*
  ✗ *Last night we had ~~the~~ dinner in a pizzeria.*
- we use *a* or *the* before meals when we describe a meal
  ✓ *Michelle always has **a** big breakfast.*
  ✗ *Michelle always ~~has big~~ breakfast.*

3 Find and correct five incorrect sentences with *a* and *the* + meals.

1 My favourite meal is ~~the~~ dinner but I eat ˄ *a* big breakfast too.
2 I get up early in the morning and I have a breakfast.
3 I celebrate my birthday with a big birthday dinner.
4 The breakfast is the most important meal of the day.
5 There is a nice park where we can have a lunch.
6 My parents often go to sleep after dinner.
7 Juliette has hot lunch in the school canteen.
8 Do you have a lunch at home or at school?

5 Animal world

Vocabulary

Animals

1 ★ **Find 12 more animals in the wordsnake.**

2 ★★ **Look at the picture. Complete the text with animal words.**

Here is my fantasy animal. It has got a ¹ _____shark_____ 's mouth, a ² _____ 's nose, a ³ _____ 's head, a ⁴ _____ 's ears, a ⁵ _____ 's neck, a ⁶ _____ 's tail, a ⁷ _____ 's front legs, a ⁸ _____ 's back legs, and a ⁹ _____ 's body. What's its name? BORIS!!

3 ★★ **Write the animals in the box next to the correct definitions.**

| polar bear   horse   ~~frog~~   shark |
| cow   dog   gorilla   cat |

1 This green animal comes out at
night.   _____frog_____
2 This fish can attack people.   _____
3 This farm animal gives milk.   _____
4 This wild animal lives in Africa.   _____
5 This pet sleeps a lot.   _____
6 This animal lives in very cold places. _____
7 You can ride this animal.   _____
8 This animal is man's best friend.   _____

4 ★★ **Complete the sentences with your own ideas about animals.**
1 Do you like cats or dogs? _I prefer dogs – they're_
very friendly .
2 I love _____ .
3 My favourite farm animal is _____ .
4 I don't like _____ .

5 ★★ **Check the meaning of these words in a dictionary. Then label the cat.**

| fur   claws   paws   whiskers   ~~tail~~ |

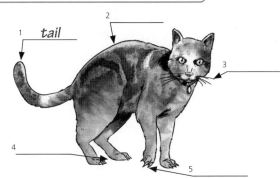

6 ★★★ **Choose an animal you like. Find a photo or draw it. Use your dictionary to label the picture.**

Language focus 1

Present continuous: affirmative and negative

1 ★ **Look at Sam's photos from the zoo. Complete the sentences with the correct form of the present continuous. Use the verbs in the box.**

| play   stand   swim   look   watch   ~~sleep~~ |

1 The lions *are sleeping* in the sun.
2 The baby gorilla _____ in a tree.

3 I _____ at a tarantula.
4 We _____ the monkeys eat their lunch.

5 The polar bears _____ in their pool.
6 He _____ next to a baby elephant.

2 ★★ **Look at the sentences in Exercise 1. Correct the false sentences below.**

1 The lions are fighting. ✗
The lions aren't fighting. They're sleeping.

2 The baby gorilla is eating its lunch.
_____

3 I'm drawing a tarantula.
_____

4 The monkeys are drinking.
_____

5 The polar bears are swimming.
_____

6 He's sitting on a baby elephant.
_____

Present continuous: questions and short answers

3 ★★ **Put the words in the correct order to make questions. Then complete the answers.**

1 homework / Are / doing / you / your / ?
Are you doing your homework?
No, I *'m not* .
I *'m reading a magazine* .

2 playing / Mark / Is / football / ?
_____
No, _____ .
He _____

3 we / having / picnic / Are / a / ?
_____
No, _____ .
We _____

4 ★★ **Complete the conversation with the present continuous form of the verbs.**

Alex: Are these your photos of the Safari Park?
Joel: Yes. Have a look! Here are the lions. They ¹ *'re watching* (watch) us, but they ² _____ (not do) anything. In this photo, the baby lions ³ _____ (fight)! Aren't they cute?
Alex: ⁴ _____ (you walk)?
Joel: No, of course not! The animals are wild! We ⁵ _____ (drive) through this section.
Alex: Oh! Right!
Joel: And here I ⁶ _____ (look) at a snake.
Alex: Oooh! What ⁷ _____ (your mum do)?
Joel: Nothing! She ⁸ _____ (run) away!

Explore adverbs of movement

5 ★★ **Ben's cat is very clever! Match the things it can do with the pictures.**

| Jump up!   ~~Run round and round!~~ |
| Look left!   Come down! |

1 *Run round and round!*   **2** _____

3 _____   **4** _____

Listening and vocabulary

Action verbs

1 ★★ **Complete the sentences with the correct form of the verbs in the box.**

| jump   hide   ~~hunt~~   fly   swim   fight   swing |

1 The man <u>_is hunting_</u> a lion.

2 The monkeys _____ in the tree.

3 The cats _____ in the garden.

4 The snakes _____ in the bath.

5 The frog _____ in the kitchen.

6 The bird _____ in the bedroom.

7 The tigers _____ in the garden.

2 ★★★ **Name two animals that:**

1 fight   _tiger_   _cat_
2 jump   _____ _____
3 swim   _____ _____
4 fly   _____ _____
5 hunt   _____ _____
6 hide   _____ _____
7 play   _____ _____

Listening

3 ★ 🔊 **07 Listen to an interview with a man with an unusual job. Tick (✓) the animals he mentions.**

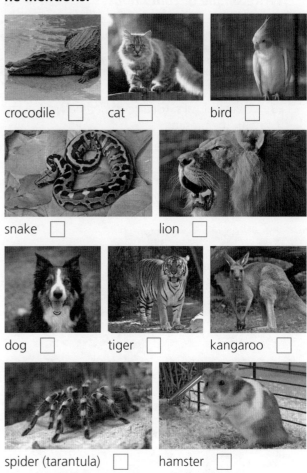

crocodile ☐   cat ☐   bird ☐

snake ☐   lion ☐

dog ☐   tiger ☐   kangaroo ☐

spider (tarantula) ☐   hamster ☐

4 ★★★ 🔊 **07 Listen again and** ⟨circle⟩ **the correct options.**

1 Steve works in **Liverpool / London**.
2 Some people have got strange animals in their **cars / houses**.
3 Steve's job is to take these animals **home / to a zoo**.
4 Pets can sometimes escape, for example **spiders / tigers**.
5 The presenter **likes / doesn't like** snakes.
6 Steve wants to buy his daughter **a tarantula / a hamster**.

Language focus 2

Present simple vs. present continuous

1 ★ **Complete the rules in the grammar table. Write *simple* or *continuous*.**

1	To talk about facts, habits and routines, we use the present _____ .
2	To talk about an action in progress, we use the present _____ .
3	We use *always*, *usually*, *sometimes* and *never* with the present _____ .
4	We use *now* and *at the moment* with the present _____ .

2 ★★ ⟨Circle⟩ the correct options in the text.

Mousehole Wild Bird
Hospital & Sanctuary

Hi, my name's Sue. At the moment I ¹ **work /
'm working** at the Mousehole Wild Bird Hospital
in my school holidays. It's a great job! The Hospital
² **accepts / is accepting** about 1,500 wild birds
every year. At the moment we ³ **look / 're looking**
after more than 100! Mousehole is on the coast,
so we've got a lot of sea birds. This is my favourite
bird, Billy. He's got a bad wing, so the vet ⁴ **looks /
is looking** at him now. I ⁵ **feed / 'm feeding** Billy
fish so he ⁶ **doesn't bite / isn't biting** the vet.
Wild birds can sometimes be aggressive! A lot of
people ⁷ **visit / are visiting** the hospital every year,
especially in the summer. We always ⁸ **explain / are
explaining** what we do to help the birds. Come
and visit us! We open every day and it's free.

3 ★★ **Write the correct form of the verb in each pair of sentences.**

play
1 Today I _'m playing___ with my uncle's dog, Patch.
2 I always ___*play*___ with Patch at the weekend.
lie
3 Every day after school I _____ on my bed and read a book.
4 Look! The cows in that field _____ down.
eat
5 Large spiders _____ frogs and other small animals.
6 Oh! The cat _____ our dinner! Do cats like spaghetti?
swim
7 In this photo a group of dolphins _____ next to our boat. Amazing!
8 Dolphins _____ quite fast, up to 32 km an hour.

Ⓔxplore the suffix *-er*

4 ★★ **Complete the sentences with the *-er* form of the words in brackets.**
1 Marina is a beautiful ___*dancer*___ . She was in the show last year. (dance)
2 My mum is a very hard _____ . She never stops! (work)
3 Would you like to be in my band? I play the guitar and you can be the _____ . (sing)
4 Who is in that car? I can't see the _____ . (drive)
5 Class, Miss White is your _____ today because Miss Smith is sick. (teach)
6 This box is very big! I need a _____ . (help)

5 ★★ **Complete the sentences with the present simple or present continuous. Use the verbs in brackets or your own ideas.**
1 At the weekend I usually _____ _____ . (do)
2 At the moment I _____ _____ . (read)
3 My friends and I sometimes _____ _____ . (go)

Reading

1 ★ **Read the text below and (circle) the correct options.**

1 Lynn Rogers is …
  a a scientist   **b** a teacher

2 The bear in the picture is …
  a a baby   **b** an adult

A life with bears

In the *forests* of Minnesota in the USA live thousands of black bears, and Lynn Rogers visits them. Lynn is an American biologist. He studies *wild* black bears. He spends a lot of time with them. He takes them food, and walks and plays with them.

Black bears are *medium-sized*, but can kill a person. A lot of people are frightened of them. But Lynn says they never hurt him or his assistants. He gives all the bears names. In this photo, Lynn is sitting in the forest with Duffy, an adult male. Male bears live alone.

Female bears live with their *cubs*, in a *den*. When Lynn *approaches* a den he says 'It's me, bear, it's me.' When the bears see him, they say a bear 'hello'. It's incredible! With Lynn's work we are learning about bear habits. He says people and bears can live together in the modern world. So now they are introducing black bears into other forests in the USA.

2 ★★ **Match the words in *bold italics* in the text with the definitions.**

1 baby bears   _____

2 places where there are a lot of trees _____

3 not big or small   _____

4 a bear lives here   _____

5 (an animal) that cannot live with people   _____

6 goes to something or somebody _____

3 ★★ **Read the text again. Are these sentences true or false? Correct the false sentences.**

1 Black bears live in Minnesota. ✓

_____

2 Lynn doesn't give the bears food.

_____

3 The bears never attack him.

_____

4 Lynn has got names for one or two bears.

_____

5 All black bears live in big family groups.

_____

6 Lynn talks to the bears.

_____

7 Lynn thinks bears and humans can't live together.

_____

4 ★★★ **Complete the summary of the text.**

Lynn Rogers is an American [1] *biologist* who studies black [2]_____ . He goes to the [3]_____ to visit them and he gives them [4]_____ . He says black bears never [5]_____ him. When he visits the female bears' [6]_____ he sometimes talks to them. We are [7]_____ a lot about bears from Lynn's work.

5 ★★★ **What new things do you learn about black bears in the text? Write them down.**

> **READING TIP**
>
> To help you remember a text, read it and write down the new information that you learned from the text.

Writing

A description of an animal

1 Read the text. Does Tom like his grandmother's cat?

My grandmother's cat

My grandmother's got a cat. His name's Ginger and he's a tabby. He's orange and white and he's got beautiful green eyes. He's got big ears and a nice long tail.

Cats are good pets because they're quite lazy and Ginger's very lazy! He sleeps all day! My grandmother's got a garden and Ginger goes out for a walk every day to hunt birds. He waits for a bird to come into the garden and then he jumps on it. Don't worry – birds are very fast and Ginger's very slow!

Cats love playing and Ginger's favourite thing to play with is a toy mouse. He's very funny when he jumps on the mouse. I love playing with Ginger and my grandmother loves him.

By Tom Davis

2 Read the text again. Are the sentences true (*T*) or false (*F*)?

1 Ginger is Tom's cat.   ____
2 Ginger's tail is long.   ____
3 He's very active.   ____
4 Ginger hunts birds in the garden. ____
5 Ginger is good at killing birds.   ____
6 Tom thinks Ginger is funny.   ____

3 Match the adjectives in the box with their opposites.

| active ~~fast~~ short small gentle |

1 slow   ___*fast*___
2 lazy   _____
3 big   _____
4 long   _____
5 dangerous   _____

4 Rewrite the sentences. Put the adjectives in the correct place.

1 He's got eyes. (beautiful)
  He's got beautiful eyes.

2 He's a dog. (lazy)
  _____

3 He's got ears. (big)
  _____

4 He's got legs. (short)
  _____

5 He's a cat. (fat)
  _____

6 He's a runner. (slow)
  _____

> **WRITING TIP**
>
> Use modifiers (*very, really, quite*) before adjectives to make your writing interesting.
> *It's a **really** fat cat.*

5 Put the words in the correct order to finish the sentences.

1 She's big/quite.
  She's quite big.

2 He's got really/eyes/big.
  _____

3 It's got ears/very/small.
  _____

4 She's lazy/quite.
  _____

5 He's a fast/very/runner.
  _____

6 He's a funny/animal/really.
  _____

Writing

> **WRITING TIP**
>
> Make it better! ✓ ✓ ✓
> We use the plural to talk about things in general.
> *Monkeys are very noisy.*

6 (Circle) the correct options.

1 Cats are / Cat is very lazy animals.
2 My uncle's got a cow / cows with a short tail.
3 Cows have got very long tails / a tail.
4 A gorilla is a wild animal. / Gorillas are wild animals.
5 There's a polar bear / polar bears in the zoo in my city.
6 I don't like spiders / the spiders.

> **WRITING TIP**
>
> Make it better! ✓ ✓ ✓
> Say why you are writing about the animal – give your opinion about it.

7 **Look back at Tom's text. Why did he write about his grandmother's cat? What's his opinion of him?**

8 **Read the sentences about different animals. Which one does <u>not</u> say why the person is writing about it?**

1 Gorillas are amazing animals. They're very big and strong.
2 My aunt's dog is very lazy but I think he's very funny.
3 Giraffes have got very long necks and they're quite slow.
4 I really like frogs – I love the different colours.

9 **Read the text again. Complete the table.**

animal	grandmother's cat
name	
physical characteristics	
daily activities	
reason for writing about the animal / opinion	

PLAN

10 **Make notes about a pet for the topics in the table in Exercise 9.**

WRITE

11 **Write a description of your favourite pet. Look at page 63 of the Student's Book to help you.**

_____
_____
_____
_____
_____
_____
_____
_____
_____
_____
_____
_____

CHECK

12 **Check your writing. Can you say YES to the questions?**

- Are the topics from Exercise 9 in your article?
- Are there different adjectives and are they in the right order?
- Do you say why you are writing about this animal?
- Are the spelling and punctuation correct?
- Do you use the plural to say general things about the animals?

Do you need to write a second draft?

Vocabulary
Animals

1 Use the clues to complete the crossword.

across

2 It's got sharp teeth. It lives in the ocean. It eats fish.

3 It's got eight legs. Some can be very dangerous.

6 It's a big orange and black cat.

8 It's grey. It eats leaves and fruit. It's got big ears. It lives in Africa and Asia.

9 It's got a very long neck. It eats leaves from trees. It lives in Africa.

down

1 It's similar to a horse. It's got black and white stripes.

4 It's got four legs. It's white. It eats fish. It lives in the Arctic.

5 It's small and green and likes water.

7 It eats grass. It's white or black. It's got a warm coat.

Total: 8

Action verbs

2 Complete the sentences with the words in the box.

> fighting   swimming   hiding
> jumping   ~~hunting~~   flying   swinging

1 The cat is __hunting__ for a mouse.

2 The dolphins are _____ in the sea.

3 The young lion is _____ with an old lion.

4 The birds are _____ over the ocean.

5 The tiger is _____ behind a tree.

6 The kangaroo is _____ over a fence.

7 The monkeys are _____ in the trees.

Total: 6

Language focus
Present continuous

3 Look at the pictures and complete the sentences, questions and short answers.

1 **A:** What __is__ the monkey __doing__ ? (do)
   B: It _____ a banana. (eat)

2 **A:** _____ the cat _____ ? (sleep)
   B: Yes, it _____ .

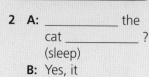

3 **A:** _____ they _____ TV? (watch)
   B: No, they _____ . They _____ at the fish. (look)

4 **A:** What _____ he _____ ? (do)
   B: He _____ a photo of an elephant! (take)

Total: 8

Present continuous vs. present simple

4 **Complete the mini-dialogues with the correct form of the verbs in the box.**

watch   play   ~~do~~   drink   do   drink   play

A: What ¹____is____ Rosie ____*doing*____ now?
B: She usually ²_____ tennis after school, but today she ³_____ her homework.

A: ⁴_____ they usually _____ coffee after lunch?
B: Yes, they do, but today they ⁵_____ tea.

A: ⁶_____ Jimmy _____ TV at the moment?
B: No, he isn't. He ⁷_____ computer games.

Total: 6

Vocabulary builder

5 **Circle the correct words.**
1 The teacher wrote the word on the (board) / pencil sharpener.
2 People from Istanbul speak **Turk / Turkish**.
3 Your father's brother is your **uncle / cousin**.
4 My grandma's hair isn't dark, it's **straight / fair**.
5 I **do / go** karate every Friday.
6 We play football **on the playing field / in the IT room**.
7 Monkeys love eating **butter / bananas**.
8 I usually eat **breakfast / dinner** at 7.30 in the morning.
9 There are lots of **fish / zebras** in the sea.
10 The children are **flying / swinging** in the tree.
11 **Gorillas / Polar bears** live in the Arctic.
12 The spider is **hiding / flying** behind a tree.

Total: 11

Language builder

6 **Complete the conversation with the missing words. (Circle) the correct options.**

Lee: Hi, Jenny. Where are you?
Jenny: I'm at the zoo with my sister. We ¹___ the dolphins.
Lee: Oh! That's nice! What ²___ doing?
Jenny: They ³___ out of the water. They're so cute. ⁴___ doing?
Lee: I ⁵___ my dad in the garden. ⁶___ a lot of birds. We're giving ⁷___ some food.
Jenny: ⁸___ often come into your garden?
Lee: Yes, they ⁹___ . But sometimes the cats ¹⁰___ them.
Jenny: Oh no! That's terrible. ¹¹___ stop them?
Lee: No, not really!

1	(a) are watching	b are watch	c watch
2	a they are	b are they	c do they
3	a is jump	b jump	c are jumping
4	a What you are	b What are you	c What do you
5	a help	b am help	c am helping
6	a There are	b There is	c There has
7	a it	b him	c them
8	a Do they	b Are they	c They are
9	a are	b do	c have
10	a attacks	b attack	c attacking
11	a You can	b Do you can	c Can you

Total: 10

Speaking

7 **Complete the conversation with the words in the box.**

take   ~~get~~   on   turn   then

A: Excuse me. How do I ¹____*get*____ to the toilets?
B: Walk down the hall and ²_____ right.
A: Down here and right. OK, ³_____ what?
B: ⁴_____ the stairs down to the first floor.
A: Down the stairs?
B: Yes, they're ⁵_____ the left.

Total: 4

Total: 53

Present continuous

With the present continuous, remember:

- to use **be** in affirmative sentences.
  - ✓ We **are** going to the shopping centre.
  - ✗ ~~We going~~ to the shopping centre.
- to use the word order **Wh- + be** + subject + **ing** in questions.
  - ✓ What **is** the gorilla doing?
  - ✗ What ~~the gorilla is~~ doing?

1 Find and correct four more mistakes.

Rob: Hey! What ~~you are doing~~ _are you doing_∧ here? Mum and Dad are waiting for us!

Ian: I'm watching the birds of prey show. It's amazing. Can you see the eagle over there?

Rob: Oh, yes!

Ian: Look! It flying to the man with the meat in his hand. Here it comes!

Rob: Wow, that's impressive! He's got the meat!

Ian: Yes, he's eating it very quickly.

Rob: Hey, look over there. Those birds are preparing to fly. Here they come! Where they are going?

Ian: They're flying in a circle. They're so colourful!

Rob: The man in the middle is calling to them. He telling them to land. Look, here they come!

Ian: What a show! I want to work at the zoo with the animals. It's great fun! Hey, where are you going?!

Rob: I'm going to the car, come on! Mum and Dad waiting.

Ian: Oh, OK. I'm coming.

Present simple vs. present continuous

Remember that:

- we use the present simple to talk about facts, habits and routines
- we use the present continuous to talk about actions in progress at the time of speaking
- we don't usually use these verbs in the present continuous:
  - be   have (for possession)   like   love   want   need

2 (Circle) the correct words.

Hi Martin,

What ¹_do you do /_ (are you doing) today? My brothers and I ²_like / are liking_ animals, so we always go to the zoo in the summer holidays and we always ³_are having / have_ a great time. We love going to the zoo! And we ⁴_are going / go_ today! At the moment, my dad ⁵_makes / is making_ packed lunches for us all and my mum is waiting for us in the car, so I haven't got much time. I need to ask you if you ⁶_are wanting / want_ to come to my house tonight. It's my dad's birthday and we usually ⁷_have / are having_ a barbecue in the garden. I hope you can come!

Bye!

Nick

Spell it right! Regular plural nouns

Remember that:

- we add **-s** to most singular nouns to make them plural
  - computer → computers   apple → apples
  - tiger → tigers
- we add **-ies** when a singular noun ends in consonant + **-y**
  - city → cities ~~citys~~   baby → babies
- we add **-es** when a singular noun ends in **-ch**, **-sh**, **-ss**, **-x** or **-z**
  - sandwich → sandwiches ~~sandwichs~~
  - class → classes   box → boxes

3 Write the plural forms of these nouns.

1	husky	_huskies_	6	class	_____
2	address	_____	7	family	_____
3	city	_____	8	tiger	_____
4	box	_____	9	bear	_____
5	lunch	_____	10	sandwich	_____

6 City life

Vocabulary

Places in a town 1

1 ★ Put the letters in order. Write the words under the correct pictures.

> astek akpr   bolwgin lyela   ptsosr nterce
> ~~nameic~~   rpotss usdatim   hposgnip ecentr
> kamert   sumume

1 ___cinema___   2 _____   3 _____

4 _____   5 _____

6 _____   7 _____   8 _____

2 ★★ Where can you do these things? Write places from Exercise 1.

1 watch a football match or see a concert
   _____sports stadium_____

2 buy some new jeans (2 places)
   _____   _____

3 see a film
   _____

4 play tennis or do a yoga class
   _____

5 go on a school trip to look at historical objects
   _____

6 practise jumps on a skateboard
   _____

3 ★★ Complete the text with places from Exercise 1.

My town is really boring! The only thing we can do is play in the street, but we don't enjoy it in the rain. We haven't got a ¹_____ , so I can only watch films on TV or online. There's a street ²_____ on Fridays in the town square, but I'm at school, of course. We haven't got a ³_____ , so, for things like new jeans or trainers, I need to go to another town by bus. There's a ⁴_____ where I sometimes play tennis, but it's quite expensive. My friends and I play on our skateboards in the street, so we're asking for a ⁵_____ , but I think it's impossible. When I'm bored, my mum always says the same: 'Visit the Pencil ⁶_____ , it's free and it's interesting.' For her, maybe, but do you want to know the history of PENCILS? I don't!

4 ★★★ Where do you go in your free time? Complete the sentences.

I love going to _the Saturday market. The clothes_
_are great_____ .
I go to _____ every week.
I like going to _____ .
I never go to _____ .
I usually go to _____ at the weekend.
The _____ is expensive.
I sometimes go to _____ in another town.

Language focus 1

was / were

1 ★ (Circle) the correct words in the grammar table.

1	I, He, She, It **was / were** there.
2	You, We, They **was / were** there.
3	He **wasn't / weren't** there.
4	**Was you / Were you** there?

2 ★ Read the blog. (Circle) the correct words.

Until recently, in Stratford, east London, the river ¹(was) / were dirty and the buildings ²was / were old and empty. It ³wasn't / weren't a nice place. But in 2012 Stratford ⁴was / were the home of the London Olympics. We ⁵was / were surprised because Stratford ⁶was / were completely different. The Olympic Park ⁷was / were new and green, and I ⁸was / were very excited!

there was/were

3 ★★ Complete the sentences with the correct form of *there was* or *there were*.

1 In 2012 _*there were*_ big celebrations in London for the Olympics. ✓
2 Before the Olympics _____ any modern buildings in Stratford. ✗
3 _____ a lot of interesting things at the museum. ✓
4 _____ a sports centre for young people in my village until recently. ✗
5 _____ an important match at the football stadium on Sunday. ✓
6 _____ many people at the new shopping centre. ✗

4 ★★ Complete the questions with *was* or *were*. Then write short answers.

1 _Were_ The Beatles popular in the 1960s?
   Yes, they were.
2 _____ Lionel Messi the first man on the Moon?
   _____
3 _____ the 2008 Olympic Games in Beijing?
   _____
4 _____ there supermarkets in ancient Rome?
   _____
5 _____ there the Internet in 1950?
   _____

5 ★★ Complete the questions with *was* or *were*. Then write the answers for you.

1 Where _were_ you yesterday afternoon at three o'clock?
   I was at home.
2 What _____ your favourite TV programme when you _____ small?
   _____
3 How many people _____ there in your class at primary school?
   _____
4 How old _____ you in 2011?
   _____

6 ★★★ Write a Fact Quiz. Write questions and answers like the ones in Exercise 4. Use *was* and *were*.

Was Pompeii in ancient Greece? No, it wasn't.

(E)xplore extreme adjectives

7 ★★ Try to improve your writing by using extreme adjectives. Replace the words in **bold** with the words in the box.

boiling   enormous   ~~ancient~~
amazing   terrified

OUR HOLIDAY: DAY 4

We went to see some ¹**really old** _ancient_ buildings – a castle and a museum. The castle was ²**very good** _____ . It had some ³**very big** _____ rooms with very beautiful pictures on the walls. It was ⁴**very hot** _____ outside but inside the castle the rooms were nice and cool. We walked up lots of stairs outside to the top. It was very high. My mum was ⁵**very scared** _____ .

Listening and vocabulary

Places in a town 2

1 ★ **Complete the places with the words in the box.**

port ~~station~~ park stop (x2)

1 bus ___*station*___
  or bus _____
2 ferry _____
3 tram _____
4 car _____

2 ★★★ **Look at the map. Complete the text with *in front of, behind, next to* and *opposite*.**

This is the centre of Springwood. You can take the tram into the centre. The tram stop is ¹ ___*opposite*___ the train station and there's a bus stop ² _____ the station. If you go by bike, you can park it ³ _____ the bus stop at the station. The sports stadium is ⁴ _____ the station and there's a car park ⁵ _____ it. When we go to the cinema, which is ⁶ _____ the sports stadium, we park there. There's a very good fruit and vegetable market ⁷ _____ the cinema. The local museum is ⁸ _____ the train station, ⁹ _____ the tram stop. It's got some very interesting things and there's a place selling delicious ice cream ¹⁰ _____ it.

Listening

3 ★ 🔊 08 **Listen to Jake talking to his aunt about a weekend trip with his parents. Circle the correct answers.**

1 Where were Jake and his parents?
  up a mountain / in a city / (in a village).
2 Who likes the place now?
  Jake / his parents / his aunt
3 Who doesn't like the place now?
  Jake / his parents / his aunt

20 years ago

Now

4 ★★ 🔊 08 **Listen again and answer the questions.**

1 Where is the village?
  In the mountains.
2 When were Jake's parents there before?
  _____
3 How many shops were there then?
  _____
4 Why was Jake happy?
  _____
5 Where were the young people?
  _____
6 Where was there wi-fi?
  _____

Language focus 2

Past simple: regular verbs

1 ★ **Write the past simple form of the verbs in the table.**

watch	shop	live	study	play
watched				

2 ★ **Complete the sentences with the past simple form of the verbs in brackets. Are the sentences true or false?**

1 Roman children ___*played*___ board games similar to games we play today. (play) ___*True*___
2 The ancient Chinese _____ the Sun, Moon and stars. (study) _____
3 In 1969 the world _____ Neil Armstrong walk on the Moon. (watch) _____
4 Armstrong and Buzz Aldrin _____ on the Moon for about 20 hours. (stay) _____
5 Christopher Columbus _____ in the Bahamas in 1692. (arrive) _____
6 Columbus _____ to go to India, not America. (plan) _____
7 Barack Obama _____ his bedroom every day when he was a child. (tidy) _____
8 The Vikings _____ America in about the year 1000. (discover) _____

Past simple: irregular verbs

3 ★ **Write the infinitive form of the past simple verbs in the table.**

do							
did	ate	got	went	had	put	saw	took

4 ★★ **Complete the text with the past simple form of the verbs in Exercise 3.**

Last month I ¹ ___*went*___ to Paris by train with my mum. We ² _____ a lot of fun things. We ³ _____ the *Mona Lisa* in the Louvre Museum, and the Eiffel Tower, and we ⁴ _____ a boat down the River Seine at night. I ⁵ _____ a lot of crepes with chocolate (delicious!)

I ⁶ _____ a great T-shirt (only €10!) at a street market, too. We ⁷ _____ a fantastic time and yesterday I ⁸ _____ some photos on Facebook for my friends to see.

ago

5 ★★ **Put the words in the correct order to make sentences.**

1 on holiday / I / months / ago / went / six
   I went on holiday six months ago.
2 teacher / ago / My / spoke to me / ten / minutes
   _____
3 was / It / Tuesday / three / ago / days
   _____
4 a new laptop / I / got / ago / three / months
   _____

Explore collocations

6 ★★ **Choose the correct options to complete the text.**

On our trip to London today, we went ¹_____ bus across Waterloo Bridge. When we were ²_____ the bus, we saw the London Eye. Then we went ³_____ foot the rest of the way to Covent Garden. We walked around and then we went ⁴_____ underground to Holborn to the British Museum. You can go ⁵_____ bike around the centre of London but we were very tired. We took a train back to the hotel and when we were ⁶_____ the train we talked about what to do tomorrow.

1	**ⓐ** by	**b** on	**c** in
2	**a** on	**b** in	**c** onto
3	**a** by	**b** in	**c** on
4	**a** on	**b** on the	**c** in the
5	**a** with	**b** on	**c** by
6	**a** in	**b** with	**c** on

Reading

1 ★ **Read the text about Covent Garden below. What can you do there?**

2 ★★ **Match the words in *bold italics* in the text with the definitions.**
1 One hundred years is a _____ .
2 A _____ is an area in a city or town with buildings around it.
3 _____ are people who entertain other people.
4 _____ are the people who decide how cities look.
5 An _____ is a person who designs buildings.

3 ★★ **Read the text again and answer the questions.**
1 What did the original architect call Covent Garden square?
   the Piazza
2 What did the market in Covent Garden sell?
   _____
3 When did the market move to another part of London?
   _____
4 Who didn't want Covent Garden to change?
   _____
5 What is the market now?
   _____

4 ★★★ **Complete the sentences with adjectives from the text.**
1 The history of Covent Garden is very *interesting* .
2 There was a _____ market that sold fruit and vegetables.
3 People in London loved the _____ square and its buildings.
4 Now there is an _____ shopping centre there.
5 It's a _____ place to visit in London.

5 ★★★ **Why is Covent Garden a popular place for tourists? Find two or three ideas in the text. Is there anything like this in your town?**

> **READING TIP**
>
> Don't worry if other people in your class read faster than you. It is more important that you understand all the information.

Come to
Covent Garden!

Home   Hotels   Shopping   Entertainment

Covent Garden is a popular place for tourists. It's got an interesting history. It was the first public *square* in London. The *architect*, Inigo Jones, took the idea from Italian cities, and called it the Piazza.

In the 1750s a market started there. It sold fruit and vegetables to shops all over the city. In 1830 there was one market building, but a *century* later there were more and more, because the market was big and important. There were also theatres, cafés and restaurants in the area.

In 1973 the market moved to an area of London with good transport and car parks. *Planners* wanted to build a conference centre, hotels and roads in Covent Garden, but the people of London wanted the beautiful square and historic buildings to stay. In the end, Londoners got what they wanted.

Now the first market building is an unusual shopping centre. It's got a lot of small shops. They sell artistic things – it's great for tourists! There are still theatres, including the Royal Opera House, and there's a Theatre Museum and a Transport Museum.

In the Piazza there are street musicians and circus *performers*. It's a wonderful place to visit when you come to London!

Writing

A description of a place

1 **Read the email about a holiday village. Is it a good place to stay?**

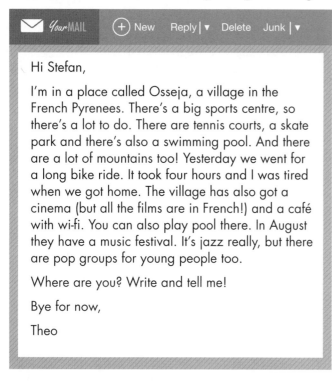

Hi Stefan,

I'm in a place called Osseja, a village in the French Pyrenees. There's a big sports centre, so there's a lot to do. There are tennis courts, a skate park and there's also a swimming pool. And there are a lot of mountains too! Yesterday we went for a long bike ride. It took four hours and I was tired when we got home. The village has also got a cinema (but all the films are in French!) and a café with wi-fi. You can also play pool there. In August they have a music festival. It's jazz really, but there are pop groups for young people too.

Where are you? Write and tell me!

Bye for now,

Theo

2 **Read the email again. Tick (✓) the places Theo writes about.**

shopping centre	☐	bowling alley	☐
museum	☐	café	☐
swimming pool	☐	tennis courts	☐
cinema	☐	market	☐
mountains	☐	sports centre	☐
sports stadium	☐	skate park	☐

Useful language Adding information

3 **Look back at the email. Write sentences with _too_ or _also_ in the correct place.**

1 You can play pool there.
You can also play pool there.

2 There are a lot of mountains.
_____

3 There are pop groups for young people.
_____

4 There's a swimming pool.
_____

5 The village has got a cinema.
_____

4 **Rewrite the sentences in Exercise 3 using _also_ in place of _too_ or _too_ in place of _also_.**

1 _You can play pool there too._

2 _____

3 _____

4 _____

5 _____

Writing

> **WRITING TIP**
>
> Make it better! ✓ ✓ ✓
> Use the infinitive without *to* after *can* and *can't*.
> *I* **can** *swim.*

5 Complete the sentences with *can* or *can't* and the verbs in brackets.

1 You _____ a lot of museums. (visit)
2 We _____ some free concerts. (see)
3 You _____ in a helicopter. (not fly)
4 We _____ tennis there. (not play)
5 I think we _____ the ferry to the island. (take)

6 Complete the sentences with *it* or *there*.

1 It's a great city. _____'s got a big sports stadium and a lot of museums.
2 _____'s a bowling alley. We can go _____ later.
3 My village is great fun. _____'s in the mountains and _____ are some great places to go cycling.
4 _____'s a great swimming pool and we can go _____ tomorrow.
5 The café's nice and _____'s got big tables.

> **WRITING TIP**
>
> Make it better! ✓ ✓ ✓
> Finish your description with a question about your friend and invite him/her to come and see you.

7 Read the sentences. Which one is <u>not</u> an invitation?

1 How are you? When are you coming to see us?
2 Where are you? Write and tell me!
3 Are you at home? Would you like to come and visit?
4 How are you doing? Why don't you come and see us?

8 Read the email again. Tick (✓) the topics that Theo writes about.

where it is ☐
its size ☐
places to visit ☐
things to do ☐
its history ☐
interesting facts ☐

PLAN

9 Choose a holiday place to write about. Use the list in Exercise 8 and make notes.

WRITE

10 Write an email to a friend describing your holiday place. Look at page 73 of the Student's Book to help you.

_____
_____
_____
_____
_____
_____
_____
_____
_____
_____
_____
_____

CHECK

11 Check your writing. Can you say YES to the questions?

- Are the topics in Exercise 8 in your description?
- Are there places from Exercise 2 in your description?
- Is there a question or invitation at the end of your email?
- Are the spelling and punctuation correct?
- Are the sentences with *can* or *can't* and with *it* and *there* correct?

Do you need to write a second draft?

Vocabulary
Places in a town 1

1 **Where am I? Write the names of the places in a town. Use the words in the box.**

> shopping centre   museum   cinema
> sports stadium   sports centre
> ~~market~~   skate park

1	I'm buying vegetables.	_market_
2	I'm choosing some new shoes.	_____
3	I'm watching a football match.	_____
4	I'm swimming.	_____
5	I'm watching a film.	_____
6	I'm looking at dinosaur bones.	_____
7	I'm using my skateboard.	_____

Total: 6

Places in a town 2

2 **Complete the sentences with the words in the box.**

> stop   ~~station~~   park   market   port

1 I'm walking to the bus ___station_ to get a bus to my friend's house.
2 I need to go to the _____ to buy some fruit and vegetables.
3 Walk to the bus _____ and wait for a number 12 bus.
4 Take the bus to the ferry _____ .
5 Meet me in the car _____ at 1.30 pm.

Total: 4

Language focus
(there) was/were

3 **Complete the sentences and questions with was, wasn't, were or weren't.**

1 **A:** Who __was___ your teacher last year?
  B: Mr Edwards.
2 **A:** _____ you at school yesterday?
  B: Yes, I _____ .
3 **A:** _____ Shakespeare a famous artist?
  B: No, he _____ .
4 **A:** Who _____ Elvis Presley?
  B: He _____ a famous rock singer.

5 **A:** _____ there a volcanic eruption here many years ago?
  B: Yes, there _____ .
6 **A:** _____ there a lot of tourists here last year?
  B: Yes, there _____ .
7 **A:** _____ there many people at the cinema last night?
  B: No, there _____ .

Total: 12

Past simple: regular and irregular verbs

4 **Complete the text with the past simple form of the verbs in brackets.**

Yesterday [1]__was___ (be) a very difficult day. I [2]_____ (get) up late and I [3]_____ (miss) the bus. I [4]_____ (go) to school by bike. The teacher [5]_____ (be) angry with me because I [6]_____ (arrive) late. He [7]_____ (give) me a lot of extra homework. It [8]_____ (not be) fair! After class I [9]_____ (play) football with my friends and we [10]_____ (forget) the time. So we [11]_____ (be) late for our class in the afternoon. Extra homework again!

Total: 10

ago

5 **Complete the sentences with ago.**

1 I went to Paris in 2013. I went to Paris __two years ago___ .
2 They visited their parents in January. They visited their parents _____ .
3 We watched a film last Monday. We watched a film _____ .
4 I ate breakfast this morning. I ate breakfast _____ .
5 She went to the skate park yesterday. She went to the skate park _____ .
6 It was boiling in August. It was boiling _____ .

Total: 5

Vocabulary builder

6 (Circle) the correct option.

1 My aunt / (cousin) is my uncle's son.
2 At school, we play basketball in the library / sports hall.
3 A banana / Milk is long and yellow.
4 I want to buy a T-shirt. Let's go to the museum / shopping centre.
5 I always wash my hair when I have lunch / a shower.
6 I've got some algebra for Maths / Music homework.
7 We went to the aquarium to see the sharks / gorillas.
8 Karen's got long wavy / tall hair.

| | Total: 7 |

Language builder

7 Complete the conversation with the missing words. (Circle) the correct options.

Lewis:	How ¹___ your weekend?
Thomas:	OK. I ²___ a football match with my mum. It ³___ my favourite team and they ⁴___ . On Sunday I ⁵___ for a pizza with my uncle. ⁶___ a good pizza place in town. It's near my ⁷___ house, so we ⁸___ there a lot.
Lewis:	⁹___ it very busy?
Thomas:	Yes! ¹⁰___ a lot of people. I had pizza, a milkshake and ¹¹___ chips.
Lewis:	I love pizza. It's ¹²___ favourite food.

1 (a) was	b are	c were
2 a watch	b watched	c watching
3 a were	b was	c are
4 a win	b winned	c won
5 a went	b go	c did
6 a There's	b There are	c They are
7 a uncle	b uncle's	c uncles
8 a eating	b are eat	c eat
9 a It was	b Were	c Was
10 a It was	b There were	c There was
11 a some	b any	c much
12 a his	b their	c my

| | Total: 11 |

Speaking

8 Put the sentences in the correct order to make the conversation.

___	a	What did you do then?
___	b	Really? What did you see?
___	c	So you didn't go to the park?
_1_	d	What did you do yesterday?
___	e	Then we went home.
___	f	First, we went to the cinema.
___	g	No, I was very tired.
___	h	We saw *Animal Park III*. After that, we had lunch.

| | Total: 7 |

| | Total: 62 |

there was/were

Remember that:

- we use *there + was/wasn't* with singular countable nouns and uncountable nouns
  there ~~were~~ an enormous amphitheatre → *there was* an enormous amphitheatre
- we use *there + were/weren't* in sentences with plural countable nouns
  there ~~was~~ two cinemas → *there were* two cinemas
- we use *there were* with *a lot of* + plural noun and *there was* with *a lot of* + singular nouns and uncountable nouns
  there ~~was~~ a lot of people → *there were* a lot of people
  there ~~were~~ a lot of traffic → *there was* a lot of traffic

1 Complete the sentences with *was* or *were*.

1 There _____*were*_____ shops, schools and markets in Pompeii.
2 There _____ milk in the fridge.
3 There _____ a lot of shops.
4 _____ there a lot of people at the cinema?
5 There _____ n't much rain.
6 There _____ a lot of interesting things to do.
7 There _____ n't any information about the museum.

Past simple: regular and irregular verbs

Remember that:

- we use *didn't* + the infinitive without *to* to make all verbs negative in the past simple. We don't use *didn't* + past simple. Remember to use the infinite without *to* of regular and irregular verbs.
  ✓ We *didn't* go to the cinema on Saturday.
  ✗ We didn't ~~went~~ to the cinema on Saturday.
- we use *don't* in the present simple, but *didn't* in the past simple

2 Make the sentences negative.

1 Peter went to school yesterday.
   Peter didn't go to school yesterday.
2 I slept for ten hours last night.
   _____
3 We travelled to Beijing on the bullet train.
   _____
4 He took the tram to the city centre.
   _____
5 David and Martin came to my party.
   _____
6 I liked visiting the museum.
   _____
7 We ate our sandwiches in the park.
   _____
8 We had a very nice time at the weekend.
   _____

Spell it right! Similar words

Be careful with these pairs of words:
thing / think
✓ What's your favourite *thing*?
✓ What do you *think* about homeschooling?
too / to
✓ He's twelve and she's twelve *too*.
✓ Natalie went *to* Japan on holiday.
were / where
✓ *Were* you at the match last night?
✓ *Where*'s the hotel?
know / now
✓ I don't *know* the answer, sorry!
✓ What are you doing *now*?

3 Circle the correct words.

1 **A:** We're going to Spain in the summer.
   B: Really! We're going there to /(too)!
2 Can you **think / thing** of something to do?
3 He wants the money **know / now**, not tomorrow.
4 I go **to / too** the sports centre on Saturdays.
5 **Were / Where** did you go last summer?
6 There are a lot of **thinks / things** to do at the sports centre.
7 Football players are celebrities – we all **know / now** them!
8 **Were / Where** Tom and Ashley at the party?

Vocabulary

Sports and activities

1 ★ **Complete the crossword. Use the pictures.**

¹ w i n d s u r f i n g

2 ★ **Write the sports from Exercise 1 with the correct verb, *play*, *go* or *do*.**

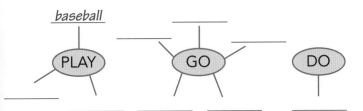

baseball _____

PLAY   GO   DO

_____ _____ _____

3 ★★ Circle **the sport which is different. Then say why. Use the clues in the box to help you.**

> individual sport   wheels   board
> ball   ~~team sport~~   water sport

1 volleyball   basketball   (skiing)
It isn't a team sport.

2 windsurfing   surfing   judo
_____

3 snowboarding   judo   volleyball
_____

4 cycling   baseball   skateboarding
_____

5 windsurfing   basketball   bowling
_____

6 surfing   skateboarding   judo
_____

4 ★★ **Complete the text with sport words from Exercises 1–3.**

I'm not very good at sport. I'm 1 m 56, so I'm not in the ¹ *basketball* team. I never go ² _____ because there is no bowling alley in my town. I don't like snow, so I don't go ³ _____ or ⁴ _____ ! I like the idea of a martial art, but there isn't a place where I can do ⁵ _____ classes. We don't live near the sea, so I can't go ⁶ _____ or ⁷ _____ , and my bike is very old, so I can't go ⁸ _____ . We sometimes play ⁹ _____ in the playground at school (not the beach!!) which is OK, but the thing I really enjoy is when I go ¹⁰ _____ in the park after school with my friends.

5 ★★★ **Which sports do you like? Write at least three sentences. Use the ideas in the box or your own ideas.**

> fun / boring / dangerous / scary
> difficult for me / easy for me

I think windsurfing is fun, but it's difficult for me.

Language focus 1

Past simple: *Yes/No* questions

1 ★ **Match the questions with the answers.**

1 Did you see my coat in the classroom?
2 Did you and Mike go skateboarding?
3 Did the school basketball team win yesterday?
4 Did you start judo classes, Anna?
5 Did your cousins go skiing at the weekend?
6 Did the PE teacher find my trainers?

a No, they didn't. They went cycling.
b No, I didn't. It was karate!
c Yes, she did. In the shower!
d No, I didn't.
e Yes, we did.
f Yes, they did: 53–44.

2 ★ **Charlie and Salma did a lot of different sports last year. Look at the table and write short answers.**

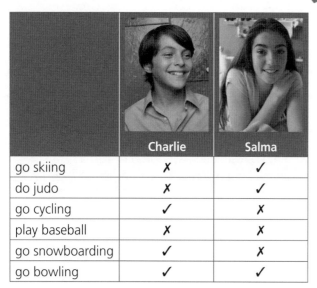

	Charlie	Salma
go skiing	✗	✓
do judo	✗	✓
go cycling	✓	✗
play baseball	✗	✗
go snowboarding	✓	✗
go bowling	✓	✓

1 Did Charlie go skiing?
   No, he didn't.
2 Did Salma do judo?

3 Did Salma go cycling?

4 Did Charlie go snowboarding?

5 Did Charlie and Salma play baseball?

6 Did Charlie and Salma go bowling?

3 ★★★ **Write questions in the past simple.**

1 you / watch / football match / last night?
   Did you watch the football match last night?
2 your parents / go / to a restaurant / last week?

3 Penny / study / Maths / last night?

4 you and your sister / go skateboarding / last summer?

5 Jason / go skiing / last winter?

4 ★★★ **Write one or two short conversations about sport. Use the questions in Exercise 3 to help you. Use *did* and *didn't*.**

Did you do PE at school today?   Yes, I did.

Explore adverbs

5 ★★ **Put the adverbs in brackets in the correct place in the sentences.**

   usually
1 I ˄ go out on Saturdays with my friends. (usually)
2 November is the month of Thanksgiving in the USA. (traditionally)
3 Professional footballers train every day. (typically)
4 People learn how to swim when they're very young. (generally)
5 We went bowling and I was good at it! (surprisingly)

Listening and vocabulary

Clothes

1 ★ **Put the letters in order to make 11 clothes words. Write the words on the correct pictures.**

> s-thrit anjes thorss risackutt
> hisstewart actjek odoihe acp
> sobot ~~routress~~ riskt

1 *trousers*
2
4
5
6
7
9
8
10
11

2 ★ **What do you usually wear in these situations? Complete the sentences.**

1 For sports at school I wear *shorts and a T-shirt or a tracksuit* .
   _____ .

2 On school days I usually wear _____
   _____ .

3 At the weekend I sometimes wear _____
   _____ .

4 For a special family celebration I wear _____
   _____ .

5 I never wear _____
   _____ .

Listening

3 ★ 🔊 **09 Listen to a conversation between two friends. Circle the correct options.**

1 Kirstie plays **basketball / baseball**.
2 The young people at the camp were from **different countries / England**.
3 The training camp was at **a university / a school** near Kirstie's home.

4 ★★ 🔊 **09 Listen again. Are these sentences true (T) or false (F)?**

1 Kirstie went to the training camp in the winter. __*F*__
2 She went on the train. ____
3 She stayed in a hostel. ____
4 She learnt about what food to eat. ____
5 Kirstie wants Gemma to see her photos. ____

5 ★★★ **Complete Gemma's diary. Use one or two words for each space.**

> I met Kirstie on my way home from school. She had a really cool ¹ __*T-shirt*__ . I asked her about it. She went to a basketball ² _____ last summer. She made friends with people from all around the ³ _____ . The camp was near Manchester and she stayed at the ⁴ _____ residence. They did a lot of exercises and they played a lot of ⁵ _____ . They learnt about healthy ⁶ _____ and studying. She's going to show me some photos at the weekend.

Language focus 2

Past simple: *Wh-* questions

1 ★ **Complete the questions with the correct word.**

1 _____*Who*_____ did you see at the party?
Patrick and Carol.

2 _____ did you eat at that restaurant?
Yesterday.

3 _____ did you get to school today?
I came by bus.

4 _____ did you play football?
In the park.

5 _____ did you do yesterday?
Not a lot. I watched TV.

6 _____ many people went swimming yesterday?
Five of us.

2 ★★ **Write past simple questions.**

1 What / you / do yesterday?
What did you do yesterday?

2 How many friends / you / see at the match?
_____

3 Where / we / go skiing last winter?
_____

4 When / Kyle / play basketball?
_____

5 Who / you / talk to at the party?
_____

6 How / they / get home last night?
_____

3 ★★★ **Read the dialogue. Write the past simple questions.**

1 Where *did you go when you were in New York?*
We went to a baseball match. It was amazing.

2 When _____?
We went on the second day of our trip.

3 Who _____?
I went with my parents and my American cousin Josh.

4 So, who _____?
I sat with Josh. He told me everything about the game.

5 How _____?
We went in the subway – the underground train.

6 What _____?
I love burgers, so I ate two!

Explore irregular plurals

4 ★★ **Read the description of words that are irregular in the plural. Write the words.**

1 When boys are adults, they are these.
m _e_ _n_

2 When girls are adults, they are these.
w _ _ _ _ _

3 Young boys and girls.
c _ _ _ _ _ _ _ _

4 The plural of *person*.
p _ _ _ _ _ _

5 Small animals, Mickey is a famous one of these.
m _ _ _ _

6 You have got these in your mouth.
t _ _ _ _ _

Reading

1 ★ **Read the text about two young world champions. What sports do they do? Where do they do them?**

2 ★★ **Complete the sentences with the words in *bold italics* from the text.**

1 9 minutes is _____ 10 minutes.
2 She _____ running – she loves it very much.
3 A person who helps other people in the mountains is a _____
4 A _____ football player plays football as a job.
5 We had a _____ and I won!

3 ★★ **Read the text again. Write *K* for Kilian, *G* for Gisela or *B* for both.**

1 His/Her parents did the same sport.   _G_
2 He/She started doing sports as a baby.   ___
3 He/She went to another place to live.   ___
4 He/She travels to a lot of different countries. ___
5 He/She teaches other people his/her sport.   ___
6 He/She went to university.   ___
7 He/She did something for the first time in 2010. ___
8 He/She can race for over 24 hours.   ___

4 ★★★ **Write the numbers from the text.**

1 He ran this many kilometres in 33 hours in the Himalayas.   _190_
2 He started ski training.   _____
3 She started kitesurfing.   _____
4 The Ultra-Trail du Mont-Blanc.   _____
5 The number of world titles she won.   _____

5 ★★★ **Think about Kilian and Gisela's lives and daily routines. Write about a day in the life of one of them.**

> **READING TIP**
>
> When you finish reading the text, answer the easy questions first and then try to answer the more difficult questions.

≫ YOUNG CHAMPIONS

Kilian Jornet was born in Sabadell in 1987. He does the extreme sport of skyrunning: running up and down mountains. His dad is a *mountain guide* and his mum is a mountain sports teacher, so Kilian learnt to ski when he was one! At six he climbed a 4,000 m mountain, and he started ski training when he was 13. Kilian won his first skyrunning *race* when he was 17. He was world champion in 2007, 2008 and 2009 and won the Ultra-Trail du Mont-Blanc (166 km) three times before he was 25. He climbed Kilimanjaro in Africa in *under* six hours (a record in 2010), and ran 190 km in 33 hours in the Himalayas near Everest.

Gisela Pulido was born in 1994. She *adores* the sea. When she was six, she watched her father kitesurf and wanted to do it too, but her parents said it was dangerous, so she didn't start until she was eight. At nine she turned *professional* and at ten she was world champion. After that the family went to live in the south of Spain. Gisela trained and studied there and went to kitesurfing competitions all over the world. In 2012 she won her eighth world title, started university and opened a kitesurf school.

Writing

A biography

1 Read the biography of Lionel Messi. How many goals did he score in one year?

My SPORTS HERO

My sports hero is Lionel Messi. He was born in Rosario in Argentina on 24th June, 1987. He was good at football but he was very small. In 1998, at the age of 11, he went to Barcelona in Spain. He played his first match for FC Barcelona in 2004 at the age of 17. Between 2004 and 2014, he played over 400 matches for his club. He won four FIFA Ballons d'Or. He has the world record for the most goals in one year (91). Before 2014 he won six leagues, two King's Cups and three Champion Leagues with FC Barcelona. He played in the FIFA World Cup finals in 2006, 2010 and 2014. At the age of 24 he became FC Barcelona's top scorer. He still plays football and he wants to win the World Cup with Argentina. I really admire Lionel Messi because he's a great footballer.

2 Read the biography again. Answer the questions.

1 When was Messi born?

_____

2 Where did he go in 1998?

_____

3 When did he play his first match with FC Barcelona?

_____

4 Which world record does he hold?

_____

5 What does he want to do in the future?

_____

Useful language Prepositions of time and place _____

3 Look back at the biography. Complete the phrases.

1 _____ Rosario
2 _____ 24th June, 1987
3 _____ the age of 11
4 _____ 2006
5 _____ Spain

Writing

4 **Match the sentence halves.**

1 My birthday is on
2 Rafa Nadal was
3 I want to compete
4 Neymar played
5 He won a gold medal in

a at the World Cup in Brazil in 2014.
b 14th March.
c 2012.
d at the Olympics in Tokyo.
e born in Manacor in Spain.

> **WRITING TIP**
>
> **Make it better! ✓ ✓ ✓**
> We can write dates like this: *2/4/2004 =*
> *2nd April 2004* or *2 April 2004*.

5 **Write the dates.**

1 31/10/2010 = *31st October 2010*
2 24/12/2014 = _____
3 8/6/1999 = _____
4 17/7/2008 = _____
5 1/1/2010 = _____

> **WRITING TIP**
>
> **Make it better! ✓ ✓ ✓**
> Say <u>why</u> you like the person you write about.

6 **Read the sentences. Which one does <u>not</u> say why the writer likes the person?**

1 Usain Bolt is an amazing athlete and a very nice person.
2 I like Angel DiMaria because he's a great footballer and he works very hard.
3 At the age of 22, she won a gold medal at the London Olympics.
4 Petra Kvitova is an excellent tennis player and I really like her.

7 **Read the biography again. Number the topics in the correct order.**

> year of birth ☐ place of birth ☐ sports ☐
> the future ☐ why he/she admires him ☐
> now ☐ teams/medals ☐

PLAN

8 **Choose a sportsperson from another country to write about. Use the Internet to find information. Make notes for each section in Exercise 7.**

WRITE

9 **Write your online biography. Look at page 85 of the Student's Book to help you.**

_____
_____
_____
_____
_____
_____
_____
_____
_____
_____
_____
_____

CHECK

10 **Check your writing. Can you say YES to the questions?**

- Are the different topics in Exercise 7 in your biography?
- Are there time expressions and dates in your biography?
- Do you say why you admire the person?
- Are the spelling and punctuation correct?

Do you need to write a second draft?

Vocabulary
Sports and activities

1 Put the letters in order to make sports words.

1 staklalbeb   _basketball_
2 frusnig   _____
3 llovyelalb   _____
4 idwngrsunfi   _____
5 oduj   _____
6 owlbgin   _____
7 glycinc   _____
8 iksnig   _____
9 dabsokatinreg   _____
10 ibanndoorwsg   _____
11 labebsal   _____

Total: 10

Clothes

2 Write the words for each picture.

1   _T-shirt_   2   _____

3   _____   4   _____

5   _____   6   _____

Total: 5

Language focus
Past simple: *Yes/No* questions

3 Circle the correct words.

Jackie: ¹(**Did you**) / **You did** go out last weekend?
Jo: Yes. We went to the sports centre and played tennis.
Jackie: ²**Were / Did** you go anywhere afterwards?
Jo: Yes, we ³**did / had**. We had an ice cream in the café.
Jackie: ⁴**Were / Did** you ⁵**saw / see** anyone there?
Jo: Yes, we ⁶**did / were**. We saw my sister and her new boyfriend.
Jackie: Ooh! ⁷**Did / Was** she see you?
Jo: No, she ⁸**not did / didn't**!

Total: 7

Past simple: *Wh-* questions

4 Put the words in order to make questions.

1   do / yesterday / What / you / did?
    What did you do yesterday?
2   wear / party / Claudia / to / did / the / What?
    _____
3   basketball / Where / you / play / yesterday / did?
    _____
4   Paul / see / film / When / did / this?
    _____
5   at / meet / Who / did / the / you / match?
    _____
6   Derek / tacos / How many / eat / did?
    _____

Total: 5

Vocabulary builder

5 Circle the correct options.

1 You can see a film at the ___ .
   a shopping centre b skate park **c** cinema
2 You can watch a football match in the ___ .
   a museum b stadium c market
3 You can travel on a river by ___ .
   a ferry b train c bike
4 You can catch a bus at the bus ___ .
   a stand b port c stop
5 You need two teams to ___ .
   a go skateboarding b play volleyball c go skiing
6 You need a board to go ___ .
   a cycling b bowling c surfing
7 You wear ___ when it's cold and wet.
   a a skirt b boots c shorts
8 You wear a ___ when it's hot.
   a T-shirt b jacket c sweatshirt

Total: 7

Language builder

6 Complete the conversation with the missing words. Circle the correct options.

Helen: Where ¹___ go yesterday?
Harry: I ²___ swimming. It ³___ fun!
Helen: Oh, ⁴___ come with you next time?
Harry: OK. But remember ⁵___ a lot of rules.
You ⁶___ a swimming cap in the pool
and you ⁷___ wear shoes or trainers
in the pool area.
Helen: ⁸___ there often?
Harry: Yes, I ⁹___ . Every Saturday. ¹⁰___ a
swimming team too.
Helen: Oh no. I ¹¹___ swim very well.

1 **a** did you b you did c do you
2 a did b went c go
3 a was b were c are
4 a I can b can I c do I
5 a there's b there are c there have
6 a doesn't wear b wear c wears
7 a don't b doesn't c do
8 a Do you go b Are you going c Did you go
9 a do b go c went
10 a There are b There's c There
11 a can't b not can c doesn't

Total: 10

Speaking

7 Complete the dialogue with the words in the box:

What happened   How was it   Cool   Really

Becky: What did you do at the weekend?
Charlotte: I went skateboarding with my brother on Saturday.
Becky: ¹_____ ! I love skateboarding.
²_____ ?
Charlotte: It was really fun. What did you do?
Becky: I went bowling with my family.
Charlotte: ³_____ ?
Becky: Yeah. It was my brother's birthday and he wanted to go.
Charlotte: ⁴_____ ? Who won?
Becky: My little sister won. She's five!

Total: 4

Total: 48

Past simple questions

> Remember, we use *did* and the infinitive in past simple questions.

1 **Are the sentences correct? Correct the incorrect sentences.**

1 Did Lynsey had a good time on holiday? ✗
   Did Lynsey have a good time on holiday?

2 Did Charlie and Salma play basketball?
   _____

3 What you have for dinner at the hotel?
   _____

4 Did they visit any monuments?
   _____

5 What time did the ski lessons start?
   _____

6 Did Susanna went to the market this morning?
   _____

7 Did she go by train or bus?
   _____

8 When you bought the plane tickets?
   _____

Past simple questions and negatives

> Remember to use *did* and the infinitive in past simple questions and negatives.
>
> ✓ **Did** you **play** basketball last weekend?
> ✗ Did you ~~played~~ basketball last weekend?
> ✓ What **did** you **do** on holiday?
> ✗ What ~~you~~ do on holiday?
> ✓ What **did** you **have** for breakfast?
> ✗ What ~~you had~~ for breakfast?
> ✓ I **didn't go** to the shopping centre yesterday.
> ✗ I didn't ~~went~~ to the shopping centre yesterday.

2 **Find and correct four more mistakes in the conversation.**

Hannah:	How was your holiday, Alisha?
Alisha:	I didn't ~~went~~ ᴬgo in the end! I didn't get to the airport and I missed the plane!
Hannah:	What? Oh no! What happened?
Alisha:	Well, we didn't get up on time. My alarm clock didn't woke me up.
Hannah:	What time was the plane?
Alisha:	Ten o'clock.

Hannah:	And what time you got up?
Alisha:	Eight o'clock!
Hannah:	So what did you do?
Alisha:	I called a taxi, but it didn't arrive for half an hour! Then I lost my bag in my house – it had all my money!
Hannah:	Oh no! Did you went to the airport?
Alisha:	No, it was now 9.30 and the airport is an hour from my house.
Hannah:	So you didn't go on holiday? What a pity! What you do for two weeks?
Alisha:	I had a holiday – at home with my cat!

Spell it right! *Clothes, shorts, trousers, jeans*

> Remember that:
> - *clothes, shorts, trousers* and *jeans* are always plural – they always end with -*s*
> - we never use *a* with *clothes, shorts, trousers* or *jeans*.
> - to talk about a single example, we use *some/any* or *a pair of*.
> ✓ I bought shorts and trousers.
> ✓ I bought **some** shorts and **some** trousers.
> ✗ I bought ~~a short~~ and ~~a trouser~~.
> ✓ He always wears black clothes.
> ✗ He always wears ~~a~~ black ~~clothe~~.

3 **Find and correct seven more mistakes.**

Jane:	Hi, Rory, what did you do yesterday?
Rory:	I went shopping with my mum to buy ~~a~~ new clothes because I'm going to a sports camp next week.
Jane:	Cool! What did you buy?
Rory:	I bought some new jeans, a short for the beach, and some shorts for tennis, a new trouser for skateboarding, three T-shirts and a tracksuit. Well, my mum bought them!
Jane:	Wow! That's a lot of new clothes! What colour are your new jeans?
Rory:	Blue, of course. I always wear a blue jean!
Jane:	Do you wear special short for tennis?
Rory:	Yes. But some people wear a white trouser.
Jane:	And what do you wear when you're not doing sports?
Rory:	Oh, nothing unusual. Just jean and a T-shirt. I'm not really interested in a clothe.

8 Holidays

Vocabulary

Seasons and weather

1 ⭐ **Find 12 more words for the weather and the seasons in the wordsquare.**

c	l	o	u	d	y	t	o	f
l	o	a	u	t	u	m	n	r
y	t	y	n	n	u	s	p	e
d	s	t	o	r	m	y	r	m
n	s	a	w	t	c	a	k	m
i	n	s	o	i	i	g	v	u
w	o	t	j	n	n	z	r	s
q	w	i	y	i	g	t	e	p
u	y	e	r	m	o	t	e	z
i	m	p	a	d	l	o	c	r
z	s	b	f	o	g	g	y	x

2 ⭐ **Complete the text with weather words. Use the first letter to help you.**

I'm from New York City, where the climate is very different in summer and winter. In winter it's always c _old_____ and after Christmas it's usually ¹ s _____ and ² i _____ (from –12 °C to 0 °C). I like winter weather! Summer is very hot and humid, day and night. I don't like it! New York is quite ³ c _____ and ⁴ r _____ any time of the year – we've all got rain boots – but it's ⁵ s _____ 234 days of the year too. One problem is tropical storms. It's often ⁶ s _____ and ⁷ w _____ in autumn. Last year we even had tornados! And sometimes it's very ⁸ f _____ too, so you can't see the tall buildings.

3 ⭐⭐⭐ **Complete the sentences. Use the words in the box.**

> rainy stormy sunny foggy ~~icy~~
> cloudy snowy windy

Hello! Here is today's world weather in two minutes!

1 In Helsinki it's –2 °C today. It's cold and
  ___*icy*___ , so a good day to go skating!
2 In London today the weather is 12 °C. It's grey and _____ . But you don't need your umbrella – it isn't _____ .
3 In Ottawa it's cold (–1 °C) and very _____ . It's a good day to make a snowman.
4 Today in San Francisco it's very _____ . You can't see anything, so drive carefully!
5 At the moment in Kingston, Jamaica it's the hurricane season, so it's very _____ . Today it isn't rainy, but it's very _____ .
6 In Rio de Janiero it's beach weather! It's warm (28 °C) and _____ .

4 ⭐⭐⭐ **Write about the activities you do in the different seasons where you live.**

In summer I like playing volleyball on the beach.

Language focus 1

be going to

1 ★ Circle the correct words in the grammar table.

1	He's going / He going to buy a new camera.
2	We **aren't going** / **not going** to go on holiday.
3	**Is** / **Are** you going to come with us? Yes, **I'm going** / **I am**.

2 ★ Look at the pictures. Complete the sentences about the people's intentions.

Amanda

Cristina and Robin

Me

Lucas

Alicia and me

You and your family

1 Lucas ____*is going to*____ learn to ride a horse.
2 Cristina and Robin _____ be famous film stars.
3 Amanda _____ climb Mount Everest.
4 I _____ buy a laptop.
5 My family and I _____ live in the country.
6 Alicia and I _____ travel around the world.

3 ★★ Complete the interview with the actor Cristina Stuart. Use the correct form of *be going to*.

Interviewer:	What ¹ __*are*__ you __*going to do*__ (do) now the film is finished, Cristina?
Cristina:	I ² _____ (have) a break. I ³ _____ (not make) any films for a year.
Interviewer:	What about Ryan?
Cristina:	Well, he ⁴ _____ (not stop) working, but we ⁵ _____ (spend) more time together.
Interviewer:	Really?
Cristina:	Yes. And his parents and my parents ⁶ _____ (visit) us too.
Interviewer:	Ah! So ⁷ _____ you and Ryan _____ (get) married?
Cristina:	I don't know! Ask him!
Interviewer:	I know you don't like living in Hollywood, so where ⁸ _____ you _____ (live)?
Cristina:	Well, I think Ryan ⁹ _____ (buy) a house in Brazil.
Interviewer:	Oh, really? Where?
Cristina:	Are you crazy? We ¹⁰ _____ (not tell) you that!

Explore collocations

4 ★★★ Complete the text with *stay*, *spend* or *take*.

This winter, my brother John and I are going to go skiing in France for two weeks in January. We're going to ¹ ____*stay*____ in a hotel in the French Alps for a week with our parents, and then we're going to ² _____ a week with our cousins. We're going to ³ _____ at my uncle's cabin in the mountains. I'm going to ⁴ _____ my winter clothes because it will be very cold, and John is going to ⁵ _____ his camera because he loves photography. He sometimes ⁶ _____ hours outside when he wants to ⁷ _____ photos!

5 ★★★ Find a picture online or in a magazine. Plan a holiday or weekend trip there. Write at least five sentences about where you are going and what your plans are.

I'm going to Hawaii in August.

Listening and vocabulary

Landscapes

1 ★ **Complete the map with words in the box.**

> desert   lake   jungle   river   hills
> sea   beach   ~~mountains~~   forest

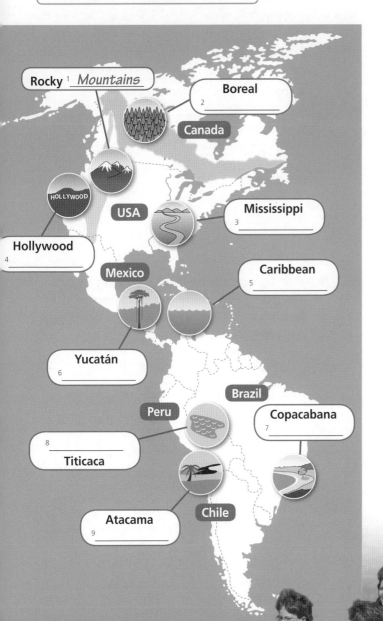

Rocky ¹ _Mountains_

Boreal
2 _____

Canada

USA

HOLLYWOOD

Mississippi
3 _____

Hollywood
4 _____

Mexico

Caribbean
5 _____

Yucatán
6 _____

Brazil

Peru

Copacabana
7 _____

8 _____
Titicaca

Chile

Atacama
9 _____

Listening

2 ★ 🔊 10 **Listen to Fernando talking about his holiday. Which sentence is true?**

a   Fernando and his family are having a boring holiday.

b   They're having a 'staycation' holiday at home.

c   They're going camping in the mountains by a lake.

3 ★★ 🔊 10 **Listen again and choose the correct options.**

1   Fernando says that on a 'staycation' …

   ⓐ you do things you can't usually do.

   b   you play games and watch TV.

   c   you haven't got time to go to sleep.

2   Fernando lives …

   a   by the sea.

   b   in the mountains.

   c   near a lake.

3   For the staycation his family …

   a   don't go out every day.

   b   made a list of things to do.

   c   made a list of fantastic holidays.

4   Tomorrow they're …

   a   having lunch at the lake.

   b   going to a museum in the morning.

   c   getting up late.

5   The next day they're …

   a   swimming in a river.

   b   going to the beach.

   c   going to the mountains.

Language focus 2

Future with *will/won't*

1 ★ Circle the correct words in the grammar table.

1	The winter **it be / will be** very cold.
2	I know I **won't / not will** pass this exam.
3	**Will you / You will** write to me when you're on holiday?

2 ★★ Write sentences using *will* or *won't*.

1 drive a car ✓
 I will drive a car.

2 get married ✗
 _____

3 go to university ✓
 _____

4 live in another country ✓
 _____

5 meet a famous film star ✗
 _____

6 speak three languages ✓
 _____

7 be famous ✗
 _____

8 live by the sea ✓
 _____

3 ★★ Complete the email with the correct form of *will* and the verbs in brackets.

> ✉ New mail
>
> Hi Alicia
>
> Just back from Greece with my family. We had an OK time, but my brother says he ¹ _won't go_ (not go) camping with my parents again next year. And he ² _____ (not visit) any more boring ruins. He says he ³ _____ (probably go) on a beach holiday with his friends. It ⁴ _____ (be) sunny and warm and they ⁵ _____ (go) swimming every day. But my parents say I ⁶ _____ (not be) old enough to go on holiday with my friends until I'm sixteen. I can't wait!
>
> How was your holiday?
>
> Write soon
>
> Amaya

4 ★★ Put the words in the correct order to make questions.

1 meet / in the park / Will / after school / you / me / ?
 Will you meet me in the park after school?

2 they / new TV / on Saturday / deliver / our / Will / ?
 _____

3 tomorrow / What / you / do / will / ?
 _____

4 be / will / next Olympics / Where / the / ?
 _____

5 the party / Will / let / to / your parents / go / you / ?
 _____

6 be / Who / live / the first person / will / on another planet / to / ?
 _____

🔍 Explore adjectives

5 ★★ Try to improve your writing by not using too many words. Rewrite the sentences. Change the parts in **bold** using the words in the box.

excellent	~~popular~~	special
luxury	perfect	amazing

1 Next year we'll stay at a beach **that a lot of people like**.
 We'll stay at a ___*popular*___ beach.

2 The water isn't too warm or too cold – **it's the best for me**.
 The water is _____ .

3 We've got horses **that are only** for learners.
 We've got _____ horses for learners.

4 The Northern Lights were **really good and surprising**.
 The Northern Lights were _____ .

5 We stayed at a hotel **which was expensive and beautiful**.
 We stayed at a _____ hotel.

6 Our ski teacher is **very, very good**.
 Our ski teacher is _____ .

6 ★★★ What are your predictions for the future? Write some things you'll do when you leave school. Write two things you won't do.

When I leave school I'll travel around Europe for six months. I won't live with my family any more.

_____

Reading

1 ★ **Read the text about two adventure holidays in Turkey. What are the main differences between Kas and Cappadocia?**

Active Holidays with Teenagers:

Turkey   Family Holidays | Teen Adventure
12yrs+ Client rating: ★★★★★

Trip type: Active
Adventure level: 4, *demanding*
Maximum group size: 16

Kas

Transport – minibus, boat, kayak, bike, quad.

Accommodation – hotel, *gulet* (2 nights).

Meals – breakfast and dinner plus lunch on gulet.

This holiday is in the town of Kas, a great place for action and adventure. You can go sea kayaking, explore by bike or quad, go *diving* or enjoy the fantastic beaches. There are excursions to beautiful forests and lakes. The holiday includes a trip on a *gulet*, a traditional sailing boat, for two nights on the Aegean Sea. We visit a small island. The friendly *crew* cooks all your meals and you can relax and enjoy a swim.

Cappadocia

Transport – minibus, horse, mountain bike, on foot.

Accommodation – hotels, camp (3 nights).

Meals – breakfast, lunch and dinner.

This holiday is an *alternative* way to *experience* Turkey. You travel by horse, bike or on foot, and camp in the mountains. We cook all your meals. You can see the famous geological rock formations of Cappadocia, visit an underground city and relax by beautiful rivers. Every day brings a new experience!

2 ★★ **Complete the sentences with the words in *bold italics* from the text.**

1 We couldn't find a bus, so we took the train as an _____ type of transport.
2 It was amazing to go snowboarding! I love to _____ new things.
3 Look! He's _____ off the rocks into the water.
4 He's got a _____ job – he has to work very hard.
5 The _____ of this ship are a nice group of people who work together.

3 ★★ **Complete the table with information from the text.**

	Kas	Cappadocia
Accommodation	*hotel + 2 nights on boat*	
Transport		
Visits		
Places		*mountains, rivers, underground city*

4 ★★★ **Which holiday are they on? Read the sentences and write Kas (*K*) or Cappadocia (*C*).**

1 'I'd like to relax on the beach today.'   *K*
2 'I don't know how to ride a horse.'   ___
3 'Can we go out on the quads today?'   ___
4 'Aren't these rocks amazing?'   ___
5 'Is there a bridge across the river?   ___
6 'How far is it to the island?'   ___

5 ★★★ **Imagine your perfect holiday. Where is it? What activities do you do there? Write three or four sentences.**

> **READING TIP**
>
> To help you organise information in a text, make notes in a table.

Writing

An email

1 Read the email. What is Marina going to do in San Gil?

2 Read the email again. Are the sentences true (T) or false (F)?

1 Marina is going to Bogotá with her family. ___
2 They're leaving very early in the morning. ___
3 They're going to stay in a hotel in Bogotá. ___
4 There are mountains and a river in San Gil. ___
5 There's nothing to do in the evening. ___

| ✉ *Your*MAIL | ⊕ New | Reply | ▼ | Delete | Junk | ▼ |

Hi Roger

Thanks for your email. I love the photos because it's nice to see your family. Did I tell you about my school trip? I'm going to Bogotá and the Andes for a week next Friday! It'll be fantastic! We're leaving at 5 am (!) because we're going to visit the city on the first day. We're going to stay in a youth hostel. All my friends are going and we're going to sleep in a room together. I can't wait!

After three days in Bogotá, we're travelling to San Gil because we're going to go rafting and hiking every morning and afternoon, then in the evening, there are activities like karaoke and a disco. What do you think? Does it sound like fun?

What about you? Has your school got a trip like ours? Are you going?

Write again soon,

Marina

Useful language Starting and finishing an email _____

3 How does Marina start and finish her email?
Start: _____
Finish: _____

4 Complete the expressions for starting and finishing an email.

1 I _____ you are well.
2 _____ are you?
3 _____ for your message.
4 _____ soon.
5 Looking _____ to _____ from you.
6 Please _____ soon.

> **WRITING TIP**
> Make it better! ✓ ✓ ✓
> Use *because* to give a reason.
> *I love the photos **because it's nice to see your family**.*

5 Look back at Marina's email. Answer the questions.

1 Why does she love Roger's photos?
_____
2 Why are they leaving at 5 am?
_____
3 Why are they going to San Gil?
_____

Writing

6 **Join the sentences with *because*.**

1 I'm going to stay in youth hostels. They're really cheap.

_____

2 We're going to the mountains. We want to go skiing.

_____

3 We're going to leave early. We want to visit the museums.

_____

4 I can't wait. All of my friends are coming too.

_____

7 **Read the sentences. Write opinion (*O*) or plans (*P*).**

1 This trip will be fantastic. ___
2 We're going to dance at the disco. ___
3 It'll be very relaxing after our visit to Istanbul. ___
4 Send the photos to Sophie – she'll love them! ___
5 My family and I are going to go to Buenos Aires for two weeks. ___

> **WRITING TIP**
>
> Make it better! ✓ ✓ ✓
> When you write about plans, say how excited you are.

8 **Put the words in the correct order to make sentences.**

1 can't / wait / I
   I can't wait.

2 fantastic / It'll / be

_____

3 best / That'll / the / be / part

_____

4 forward / really / it / I'm / looking / to

_____

9 **Read the email again. Tick (✓) the questions Marina answers.**

Where are you going? ☐
Who are you going with? ☐
How long are going for? ☐
How are you going to travel? ☐
Where are you going to stay? ☐
What are you going to do? ☐

PLAN

10 **Invent a school trip to write about. Use the questions in Exercise 9 and make notes.**

WRITE

11 **Write an email to a friend about the trip. Look at page 95 of the Student's Book to help you.**

_____

_____

_____

_____

_____

_____

_____

_____

_____

_____

_____

CHECK

12 **Check your writing. Can you say YES to the questions?**

- Did you answer the questions in Exercise 9 in your email?
- Are there expressions for starting and finishing in your email?
- Do you say why you are doing the different things?
- Do you say how excited you are?
- Are the spelling and punctuation correct?

Do you need to write a second draft?

Vocabulary
Seasons and weather

1 Complete the sentences with the words in the box. Which two words are not in the sentences?

> winter windy stormy spring icy ~~summer~~
> autumn snowy rainy cloudy sunny

1 I love __summer__ because it's hot and _____ .

2 I like _____ because it's cold and sometimes _____ .

3 I love _____ because of all the flowers.

4 We need our umbrellas every day because it's _____ .

5 I love _____ because the leaves are gold, yellow and red.

6 I don't like _____ weather because there is a lot of wind and rain.

7 I don't like _____ weather because it's dangerous to walk on the street.

☐ Total: 8

Landscapes

2 Write the names of the places.

It's a place where…

1 you can surf.   s _ea_____
2 tigers live.   j_____
3 you can catch fish.   r_____
4 you can catch fish.   l_____
5 you can climb.   h_____
6 you can see lots of trees. f_____
7 you can go snowboarding.   m_____
8 you can find sand.   b_____

☐ Total: 7

Language focus
be going to

3 Complete the sentences and short answers with the correct form of *be going to*. Use the verbs in brackets.

1 **A:** What __are you going to do__ next summer? (you / do)

   B: I _____ my cousin in Australia. (visit)

2 **A:** _____ in a hotel? (she / stay)

   B: No, she _____ .

3 **A:** _____ mountains in Switzerland? (Liz and Rob / climb)

   B: Yes, they _____ .

4 **A:** We _____ on holiday this year. (not go)

   B: Oh, what a pity!

☐ Total: 6

Future with *will/won't*

4 Complete the sentences with *will* and the verbs in the box.

> not play pass forget ~~be~~ not wear live

1 It __will be__ sunny tomorrow. Let's go to the beach.

2 When I'm older, I _____ in a big house with a garden.

3 It will be rainy tomorrow so we _____ basketball.

4 Helen _____ her new dress to the party tomorrow.

5 My mum thinks I _____ to do my homework tonight.

6 The Maths exam was hard. We don't think we _____ it.

☐ Total: 5

Vocabulary builder

5 Complete the sentences with the correct word.

1 Tigers live in the ___*jungle*___ .
   a jungle **b** beach **c** sea

2 In the winter we go snowboarding in the
   _____ .
   a river **b** lake **c** mountains

3 The weather in the desert is _____ .
   a rainy **b** snowy **c** sunny

4 It's difficult to see when it's _____ .
   a foggy **b** cloudy **c** windy

5 When it's snowy I wear _____ .
   a boots **b** shorts **c** a skirt

6 You need a ball to _____ .
   a play **b** do judo **c** go
   volleyball skateboarding

7 There are lots of _____ on my street.
   a bus stops **b** bus **c** ferry ports
   stations

8 We watched a football match at the
   _____ .
   a bowling **b** skate park **c** sports stadium
   alley

9 The birds are _____ in the sky.
   a hiding **b** swinging **c** flying

10 _____ have very big ears.
   a Elephants **b** Sharks **c** Cats

11 I ate ice cream for _____ today.
   a breakfast **b** main **c** dessert
   course

12 There is a lot of _____ on this pizza.
   a butter **b** cheese **c** rice

13 We studied mountains and lakes in _____
   today.
   a PE **b** Geography **c** Music

Total: 12

Language builder

6 Circle the correct options.

Sam: Where [1] **are you going** / do you go on
holiday this summer?

Clare: We [2] **'re going** / go to Spain. We
[3] stay / **'re going to stay** with some
friends.

Sam: Really? I [4] **went** / go to Spain last year.
The beach [5] **was** / are fantastic.

Clare: I know! What about you?

Sam: I'm not sure. We sometimes
[6] **visit** / are visiting my [7] **aunt's** / aunts
house. She [8] **lives** / live in the mountains.
[9] **There's** / There are a beautiful lake and
we [10] **can** / must go swimming there
every day.

Clare: It sounds really good!

Total: 9

Speaking

7 Put the words in order to make suggestions.

1 to / film / Where / the / shall / go / we / see?
   Where shall we go to see the film?

2 park / to / go / to / football / Let's / the / play
   _____

3 brother / don't / Canada / visit / Why / we /
   my / in?
   _____

4 Turkey / about / going / the autumn / What /
   to / in?
   _____

5 prefer / new / I'd / to / boots / a / of / buy / pair
   _____

Total: 4

Total: 51

85

be going to

Remember that:

- we use the correct form of **be + going to +** infinitive. Don't forget *be*!
  - ✓ We **are going to** visit my grandparents.
  - ✗ ~~We going~~ to visit my grandparents.
- we form questions with **be** <u>before</u> the subject.
  - ✓ **Are** you going to stay in a cabin?
  - ✗ ~~You are~~ going to stay in a cabin?

1 Put the words in the correct order to make sentences and questions. Add the correct form of *be*.

1 going to / you / take / a lot of / photos?
   <u>*Are you going to take a lot of photos?*</u>

2 going to / hotel / in / a / stay / we / luxury
   _____

3 going to / you / when / come / my / house / to?
   _____

4 going to / Sarah and I / France / go / to / this summer
   _____

5 going to / film / a / tonight / watch / not / I
   _____

6 going to / skateboarding / at the weekend / try / James?
   _____

7 going to / you / new / dress / your / wear / to / party / the?
   _____

Future with *will/won't*

Remember that:

- we use *will* + the infinitive without *to* to make predictions about the future.
  - ✓ I hope I **will see** you in the summer.
  - ✗ I hope I will ~~seeing~~ you in the summer.
  - ✗ I hope I will ~~saw~~ you in the summer.
- we use *will be* to describe something in the future. Remember to use *be*!
  - ✓ I think you **will be** very happy.
  - ✗ I think you ~~will very~~ happy.
- we use *will* + *be* or *will* + another verb. We don't use *will* + *be* + another verb
  - ✓ Maybe I **will see** you tomorrow.
  - ✗ Maybe I will ~~be~~ see you tomorrow.

2 Are the sentences correct? Correct the incorrect sentences.

1 I don't think it will raining tomorrow.
   <u>*I don't think it will rain tomorrow.*</u>

2 At this time tomorrow, John will be arrive in England!
   _____

3 I hope you will enjoyed your holiday.
   _____

4 It will be sunny in New Zealand in December.
   _____

5 It's sunny today. I think I'll going to the beach.
   _____

6 Do you think the weather will too cold in September?
   _____

7 I will be send you a postcard from Colombia.
   _____

Spell it right! Seasons and months

Remember that:

- we only write the names of seasons with a capital letter if they begin a sentence
  - ✓ My favourite season is **winter**.
  - ✓ **Winter** is my favourite season.
  - ✗ My favourite season is ~~Winter~~.
- we always write the names of months with a capital letter
  - ✗ Maria's favourite month is **February**.
  - ✗ Maria's favourite month is ~~february~~.

3 Find and correct six more mistakes.

My cousin, Sarah, lives in New Zealand and I live in England. Our lives are very different. When I have
    s
    ⌄Summer holidays, in July and August, it's Winter
in New Zealand. So, when I go to the beach, Sarah goes skiing. In Winter, when it's rainy or snowy in England, it's Summer in New Zealand. Sarah's family usually go to the beach in december for a whole month, because it's their summer holidays! And in february and march when it's the beginning of Spring for me, it's the beginning of autumn for Sarah. It's very strange!

Speaking extra

Asking for phone numbers and email addresses

1 ★ **Put the words in order to make questions.**

1 number / your / What's / phone / ?

_____

2 your / address / email / What's / ?

_____

2 ★ **Match the questions in Exercise 1 with the answers.**

a It's eddieb13@schoolemail.com ____

b It's 8451 355 7601 ____

3 ★★ 🔊 11 **Listen and write the answers.**

Conversation 1:

1 What's her phone number?

_____

Conversation 2:

2 What is Bill's email?

_____

3 What does she want to send Bill?

_____

Conversation 3:

4 What is the boy's email?

_____

4 ★ **Read the conversation. What does Clara want? Why?**

Mandy:	¹ _____ ?
Clara:	Hello, Mandy? ² _____ Clara.
Mandy:	Oh, hi, Clara. How are you?
Clara:	Fine thanks. Listen, ³ _____ your email address? I want to send you a video.
Mandy:	Oh, great! It's mandyville@schoolemail.com.
Clara:	Hold on a ⁴ _____ . I haven't got a pen! OK, say that again.
Mandy:	mandyville@schoolemail.com.
Clara:	How do you ⁵ _____ *mandyville*?
Mandy:	It's m-a-n …
Clara:	Oh, my grandparents are here! Can I call you ⁶ _____ ?
Mandy:	Err … OK, no problem. Bye, Clara.
Clara:	Bye.

5 ★★ 🔊 12 **Complete the conversation in Exercise 4 with the words in the box. Then listen and check.**

> what's   spell   Hello   second   It's   back

Focus on pronunciation: Email addresses

6 ★ 🔊 13 **How do you say these symbols and addresses? Listen and repeat.**

1 @   2 .net   3 .com   4 .co.uk

5 .tr   6 .org

7 ★ 🔊 14 **Listen to the conversation. Where is Chris?**

8 ★★★ 🔊 14 **Listen again and complete the conversation.**

Rob:	Hello?
Chris:	Hi, Rob. ¹ _____ ?
Rob:	Hi, Chris. How are you?
Chris:	Fine thanks. ² _____ ?
Rob:	I'm OK.
Chris:	Listen, ³ _____ ?
Rob:	It's robturner22@yourmail.net.
Chris:	⁴ _____ . What's the first part?
Rob:	robturner22.
Chris:	Was it .net or ⁵ _____ ?
Rob:	.net.
Chris:	OK, thanks. Oh, there's someone at the door. Can I ⁶ _____ ?
Rob:	Sure, OK. Talk to you later.
Chris:	Bye.

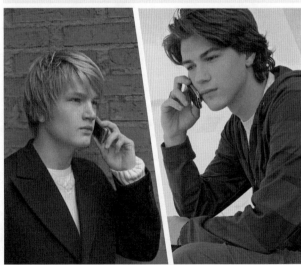

9 ★★ 🔊 14 **Listen again and check your answers. Then listen and repeat the conversation.**

Speaking extra

Asking for information

1 ★ **Put the words in order to make questions and answers.**

1 you / school / do / What / do / after / ?

_____

2 homework / I / do / After / my / school

_____

3 I / home / I / television / get / usually / When / watch

_____

4 the piano / day / after / every / I / practise / school

_____

2 ★ 🔊 15 **Listen and choose the correct answer.**

Conversation 1

1 She plays **football** / **basketball**.

Conversation 2

2 She wants to go to **tennis** / **dance** classes.

3 The classes are on Mondays and **Wednesdays** / **Thursdays**.

Conversation 3

4 The boys are talking about **Art** / **chess** classes.

5 The class on Friday starts at **5** / **6.30** pm.

3 ★ **Read the conversation. What does Jenny do on Saturdays?**

Luke:	What do you do after school, Jenny?
Jenny:	I go home, do my homework and ¹_____ .
Luke:	Do you do activities after school?
Jenny:	No, I've got a lot of ²_____ . What about you?
Luke:	Yes, I go to violin classes.
Jenny:	Really? What days are your violin classes?
Luke:	On Tuesdays and ³_____ .
Jenny:	What time are the classes?
Luke:	They're from 4.30 to ⁴_____ pm.
Jenny:	On Saturdays from 10 to 12 am I go to tennis classes.
Luke:	Oh, great. How much does it cost?
Jenny:	It's ⁵_____ a month.
Luke:	Can I come with you?
Jenny:	Yes, sure!

4 ★★ 🔊 16 **Complete the conversation in Exercise 3 with the words in the box. Then listen and check.**

£15   homework   5   Thursdays   watch TV

Focus on pronunciation: Questions

5 ★ 🔊 17 **Listen and repeat. Copy the intonation.**

1 Are you lost?

2 What do you do after school?

3 Can I come with you?

4 How much does it cost?

5 Do you know about chess classes?

6 ★ 🔊 18 **Listen to the conversation. What other class does William do? What does Chloe do?**

7 ★★★ 🔊 18 **Listen again and complete the conversation.**

William:	Hello. ¹_____ ?
Chloe:	Yes, I am. This is my first time here. ²_____ the drama classes?
William:	Yes, sure. I do drama classes too. My name's William.
Chloe:	Hi, William. I'm Chloe. ³_____ ?
William:	Sure, Chloe. It's in Room A21.
Chloe:	So do you do other activities after school?
William:	Yes, I do. On ⁴_____ I go swimming.
Chloe:	Swimming? ⁵_____
William:	They're from ⁶_____ pm.
Chloe:	How much does it cost?
William:	I think it's £20 a month.
Chloe:	Oh, I can't go on Fridays anyway. I play chess on Fridays.

8 ★★ 🔊 18 **Listen again and check your answers. Then listen and repeat the conversation.**

Speaking extra

Asking and giving permission

1 ★ **Put the words in order to make questions and answers.**

1 you / at / use / mobile / your / school / Can / phone / ?

_____

2 school / can't / our / We / in / phones / use / anywhere

_____

3 emergency / only / in / use / them / We / can / an / in school

_____

4 We / teachers / use / but / them / the / can / can't

_____

2 ★★ 🔊 **19** **Listen and write the answers.**

Conversation 1:

1 What does the girl want to play?

_____

Conversation 2:

2 How much money does the boy want to borrow?

_____

3 Why doesn't his mum give him the money?

_____

Conversation 3:

4 What does the girl want to do?

_____

5 Who can come to the girl's house on Friday?

_____

3 ★ **Read the conversation. How much money does Paul's dad give him?**

Paul:	Hi, Dad. Can I have new trainers for ¹_____ , please?
Dad:	New trainers? Why? What's wrong with the trainers you've got now?
Paul:	They're really ²_____ and ... well, I don't like them.
Dad:	Well, sorry, Paul, I'm afraid you can't.
Paul:	Why not?
Dad:	Because I haven't got money to buy new trainers. How ³_____ are they?
Paul:	They're £50.
Dad:	£50?! I'm sorry, Paul, I haven't got £50 for new trainers.
Paul:	But I ⁴_____ some money.
Dad:	Oh yeah?
Paul:	Yes, I've got £35, so can I ⁵_____ the rest?
Dad:	OK ... yes, you can.
Paul:	Great! Thanks Dad.

4 ★★ 🔊 **20** **Complete the conversation in Exercise 3 with the words in the box. Then listen and check.**

much   borrow   football   've got   old

Focus on pronunciation: Linking

5 ★ 🔊 **21** **Listen to the groups of words together. Then listen again and repeat.**

1 Can I go out tonight?
2 I'm afraid you can't.
3 Can we go swimming on Saturday afternoon?
4 Yes, you can.

6 ★ 🔊 **22** **Listen to the conversation. What does Carl want? Why can't he borrow it?**

7 ★★★ 🔊 **22** **Listen again and complete the conversation.**

Carl:	Hi, Sandy. ¹_____ your computer for a minute?
Sandy:	Oh, hi, Carl. No, sorry, ²_____ you can't.
Carl:	Oh, why not? I really need it!
Sandy:	Because I'm finishing my homework. ³_____ a few minutes.
(later)	
Carl:	Sandy, can I borrow your computer now?
Sandy:	Oh, sure ... yes, ⁴_____ .
Carl:	Thanks Sandy. ... Sandy! Can you tell me the password?
Sandy:	It's sandy.99.
Carl:	⁵_____ it?
Sandy:	S-A-N-D-Y dot 9-9.
Carl:	Great. Thanks Sandy-dot-99!

8 ★★ 🔊 **22** **Listen again and check your answers. Then listen and repeat the conversation.**

Speaking extra

Ordering food

1 ⭐ **Put the words in order to make questions and answers.**

1 do / for / What / lunch / you / have / ?

_____

2 chicken / for / I / and vegetables / usually / lunch / have

_____

3 piece / I / fruit / a / of / have / always

_____

4 pizza / My / food / is / favourite

_____

2 ⭐⭐ 🔊 **23 Listen and write the answers.**

1 What does Kevin order? _____
2 What filling does he want? _____
3 What drink does he order? _____
4 How much is it? _____

3 ⭐⭐ **Read the conversation. What do Alison and Emily order? Complete the waitress's note.**

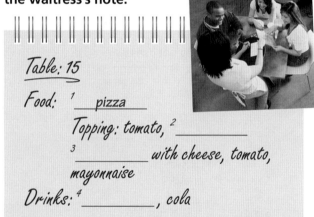

Table: 15

Food: ¹ ___pizza___
Topping: tomato, ² _____
³ _____ with cheese, tomato, mayonnaise
Drinks: ⁴ _____, cola

Waitress:	Hello. Would you like to ¹_____ now?
Alison:	Yes, please. Can I have a pizza?
Waitress:	Sure. What topping ²_____ you like?
Alison:	Err … I'd like cheese and tomato, please.
Waitress:	OK, what would you like to ³_____ ?
Alison:	Water, please.
Waitress:	OK, and what ⁴_____ you?
Emily:	Can I have a hamburger, please?
Waitress:	A hamburger. OK. What would you like on the hamburger?
Emily:	I'd like cheese, tomato and some mayonnaise.
Waitress:	Of ⁵_____ . And to drink?
Emily:	Can I have a cola, please?
Waitress:	OK, no problem.

4 ⭐⭐ 🔊 **24 Complete the conversation in Exercise 3 with the words in the box. Then listen and check.**

> would   course   drink   order   about

Focus on pronunciation: Sentence stress

5 ⭐ 🔊 **25 Listen to the orders. Mark the stress on the important words or parts of words. Then listen again and repeat.**

1 Can I have a pizza, please?
2 Can I have a hamburger, please?
3 I'd like a glass of water, please.
4 I'd like a chicken sandwich, please.

6 ⭐ 🔊 **26 Listen to the conversation. What does Howard order? Why does he change his order?**

7 ⭐⭐⭐ 🔊 **26 Listen again and complete the conversation.**

Waitress:	Hi there. What can I get you?
Howard:	Hi. ¹_____ a taco, please?
Waitress:	Sure. What ²_____ would you like?
Howard:	I'd like beef with cheese and tomato, please.
Waitress:	Do you want one or two tacos?
Howard:	Err … two please. They're quite small.
Waitress:	Right. ³_____ ?
Howard:	Yes, please. ⁴_____ an orange juice.
Waitress:	Oh, I'm sorry. We haven't got orange juice. We've got lemonade, cola or water.
Howard:	Oh, OK, water please.
Waitress:	⁵_____ . Your two beef tacos and your water.
Howard:	⁶_____ ?
Waitress:	It's £4.75, please.
Howard:	Here you are.
Waitress:	Thanks. And 25p change. Bye now.
Howard:	Bye.

8 ⭐⭐ 🔊 **26 Listen again and check your answers. Then listen and repeat the conversation.**

Speaking extra

Asking for and giving directions

1 ⭐ **Put the words in order to make questions and answers.**

1 like / Do / going / you / museums / to / ?

_____

2 art museums / Yes, / to / I / going / like

_____

3 really / zoo / love / to / I / the / going

_____

4 the / one / Science Museum / favourite / is / My

_____

2 ⭐ 🔊 **27 Listen and choose the correct options.**

Conversation 1:

1 The aquarium is on the **left** / **right**.

Conversation 2:

2 The girl wants to see the **elephants** / **monkeys**.

3 They are near the **monkeys** / **kangaroos**.

Conversation 3:

4 Turn right after the **snakes** / **tigers**.

5 The exhibit is on the **first** / **third** floor.

3 ⭐ **Read the conversation. What's in front of the Science Museum?**

Dave:	Excuse me, how do I ¹_____ to the Science Museum?
Man:	The Science Museum? Let's see … It's on Canada Avenue.
Dave:	Canada Avenue?
Man:	That's right. Go ²_____ down this street. Turn left at the end and it's the first street on your right.
Dave:	So turn left and ³_____ right?
Man:	Yes, that's it. There's a school in front of the museum.
Dave:	OK, ⁴_____ . Thank you.
Man:	You're ⁵_____ .

4 ⭐⭐ 🔊 **28 Complete the conversation in Exercise 3 with the words in the box. Then listen and check.**

> great   then   get   welcome   straight

Focus on pronunciation: Word stress in compound nouns

5 ⭐ 🔊 **29 Listen and mark the stress on the important parts of the words. Then listen again and repeat.**

1 history museum

2 parrot exhibit

3 science museum

4 art history

5 arts festival

6 ⭐ 🔊 **30 Listen to the conversation. What exhibit do Alex and Marian want to see? What exhibit do they go to?**

7 ⭐⭐⭐ 🔊 **30 Listen again and complete the conversation.**

Alex:	Wow! This is a big museum.
Marian:	Well, the Science Museum has got a lot of different exhibits. Let's get some help.
Alex:	Yes, good idea. … Excuse me, ¹_____ the Arctic Life exhibit?
Guide:	Arctic Life? Oh, I'm afraid that exhibit is closed. They're cleaning today.
Marian:	Oh dear.
Guide:	Well, why don't you go to the Animal Photography exhibit? It's ²_____ .
Marian:	Animal Photography? Is it interesting?
Guide:	Oh, yes, it is. There are amazing photos of different animals … elephants, giraffes, polar bears …
Alex:	OK, how do we get there?
Guide:	Well, ³_____ to the second floor.
Alex:	Second floor. OK, then what?
Guide:	Turn right at the top of the stairs. ⁴_____ in the main hall.
Marian:	Great. Thanks very much.
Guide:	⁵_____ .

8 ⭐⭐ 🔊 **30 Listen again and check your answers. Then listen and repeat the conversation.**

Speaking extra

Sequencing

1 ⭐ **Put the words in order to make questions and answers.**

1 do / go / Where / your friends / usually / with / you / ?

_____

2 to / shopping centre / we / Usually / go / the

_____

3 My friends / a café / usually / and I / to / walk

_____

4 the / usually / to / go / For fun / cinema / I

_____

2 ⭐⭐ 🔊 **31 Listen and put the conversation in order.**

A	**Dave:**	What did you see?	___
B	**Dave:**	Hi, Tom. What did you do at the weekend?	_1_
C	**Dave:**	Cool. What did you do then?	___
D	**Dave:**	Really?	___
E	**Tom:**	Yes. First of all we went to the shopping centre. And then after that we went to the cinema.	___
F	**Tom:**	Oh, hi, Dave. Not a lot really. We went out on Saturday.	___
G	**Tom:**	After that we went to Jacob's house to play video games.	___
H	**Tom:**	We went to see the new *Star Wars*.	___

3 ⭐⭐ **Read the conversation. Where was Harry on Saturday afternoon?**

> **Lily:** So what ¹_____ you do at the weekend, Harry?
> **Harry:** Oh, it was awful!
> **Lily:** Really? Why?
> **Harry:** ²_____ of all, on Saturday, Mark said he wanted to go to the skate park.
> **Lily:** OK … He loves skating.
> **Harry:** So we went to the skate park before lunch. ³_____ were lots of people.
> **Lily:** Cool.
> **Harry:** Then Mark went really fast and he fell off his skateboard.
> **Lily:** Oh no. ⁴_____ you went to the hospital?
> **Harry:** Yes, and we were there all afternoon! ⁵_____ that, we went to Mark's house. His mum was quite angry.

4 ⭐⭐ 🔊 **32 Complete the conversation in Exercise 3 with the words in the box. Then listen and check.**

> There   did   After   First   So

Focus on pronunciation: Chunks

5 ⭐ 🔊 **33 Listen to how we can put words in sentences into groups. Listen and circle the groups of words. Then listen again and repeat.**

1 First of all, on Saturday, we went to the skate park.
2 After that, we went to Mark's house.
3 So we went to the skate park before lunch.
4 My friends and I usually walk to a café.

6 ⭐ 🔊 **34 Listen to the conversation. Where did Olivia go yesterday?**

7 ⭐⭐⭐ 🔊 **34 Listen again and complete the conversation.**

> **Bobby:** Hi, Olivia. ¹_____ yesterday?
> **Olivia:** Hi, Bobby. It was great!
> **Bobby:** Really? What did you do?
> **Olivia:** We went to the new bowling alley in town.
> **Bobby:** Wow! Was it good?
> **Olivia:** Yeah, it was amazing. We played all afternoon.
> **Bobby:** Cool. So you liked it?
> **Olivia:** Oh yes. ²_____ we went shopping at the shopping centre. ³_____ , we went to the bowling alley.
> **Bobby:** OK.
> **Olivia:** ⁴_____ , we went to a restaurant for dinner. So what did you do?
> **Bobby:** I was in bed all weekend. It was awful.
> **Olivia:** ⁵_____ !

8 ⭐⭐ 🔊 **34 Listen again and check your answers. Then listen and repeat the conversation.**

Speaking extra

Expressing interest

1 ★ **Join the parts of the sentences.**

1 My favourite sport's swimming.
2 My favourite sport is tennis
3 I'm the captain of my team. It's a lot of fun
4 My team practises twice a week

a and we're all really good friends.
b I like being in the pool and I love winning competitions.
c and we play games on Saturday.
d because it's fast and fun.

2 ★ ★ 🔊 35 **Listen and write the answers.**

Conversation 1:
1 What sport did the girl play?

_____

Conversation 2:
2 What sport did the boy do?

_____

3 What was the problem?

_____

Conversation 3:
4 What sport did the girl do?

_____

5 Why is she unhappy?

_____

3 ★ ★ **Read the conversation. Why didn't Eric like snowboarding at first?**

Jamie: What did you do this weekend, Eric?
Eric: I ¹_____ snowboarding for the first time with my dad.
Jamie: Wow! How was it?
Eric: It was OK! I had a lot of ²_____ at first.
Jamie: Oh no! Why? What happened?
Eric: First of all, the boots were too small. And I ³_____ off the board a lot. And it was really cold!
Jamie: Really? I'm ⁴_____ .
Eric: It's OK. Dad didn't like it either. We're going windsurfing next week!
Jamie: ⁵_____ ! That'll be fantastic.
Eric: I hope so!

4 ★ ★ 🔊 36 **Complete the conversation in Exercise 3 with the words in the box. Then listen and check.**

sorry   Cool   went   fell   problems

Focus on pronunciation: Showing interest with tone

5 ★ 🔊 37 **Listen to these words. Does the speaker's voice go up or down? Then listen again and repeat.**

1 Really?   3 Oh no.
2 Cool.   4 Wow!

6 ★ 🔊 38 **Listen to the conversation. What was the score in the match? What did Sean buy at the match?**

7 ★ ★ ★ 🔊 38 **Listen again and complete the conversation.**

Ava: Hi, Sean. ¹_____ this weekend?
Sean: We went to a football match yesterday.
Ava: Really? ²_____ ?
Sean: It was great but the first half of the match was awful!
Ava: Oh no. Why? ³_____ ?
Sean: Well, the other team scored two goals at the start of the match.
Ava: So you lost?
Sean: No, it was a great game. We scored three goals in the second half. We were so happy!
Ava: Cool! ⁴_____
Sean: It was. And look, I bought the United sweatshirt.
Ava: It's very cool.
Sean: Hey, maybe next time ⁵_____ with us.
Ava: OK! I'd love to.

8 ★ ★ 🔊 38 **Listen again and check your answers. Then listen and repeat the conversation.**

Speaking extra

Making suggestions

1 ★ **Put the words in order to make questions and answers.**

1 like / Where / you / holiday / do / on / going / ?

   _____

2 to / going / the / On holiday / seaside / like / I

   _____

3 going / the Caribbean / In the summer / like / to / on holiday / I

   _____

4 go / lake / Sometimes / in / we / fishing / the

   _____

2 ★ 🔊 39 **Listen and complete the sentences.**

Conversation 1:

1 They want to practise their English in

   _____ .

Conversation 2:

2 Daniel suggests going to the _____ .

3 They decide to go swimming in the _____ .

Conversation 3:

4 They are talking about where to go in the

   _____ .

5 Grace would prefer to go to the _____ .

3 ★★ **Read the conversation. What are they <u>not</u> going to do tomorrow?**

Josh:	Where shall we go tomorrow?
Rosie:	What ¹_____ mountain biking in the morning?
Josh:	Mountain biking? I'd ²_____ not to go mountain biking.
Rosie:	Why?
Josh:	Well, because the weather forecast says it'll probably be rainy tomorrow.
Rosie:	Oh, yes. The weather ³_____ be very nice.
Chloe:	Why don't we go to your house for ⁴_____ practice?
Josh:	Cool! My mum and dad are going out tomorrow.
Rosie:	Yes, and we can practise that new song.
Josh:	That's a good ⁵_____ !
Chloe:	Do you think Louise will come?
Rosie:	Let's call her.

4 ★★ 🔊 40 **Complete the conversation in Exercise 3 with the words in the box. Then listen and check.**

> band   won't   prefer   idea   about

Focus on pronunciation: Suggestions through tone

5 ★ 🔊 41 **Listen to these suggestions. Does the speaker's voice go up or down? Then listen again and repeat.**

1 What about going to the seaside?
2 Let's go mountain biking.
3 Why don't we go to the cinema?
4 I'd prefer to watch TV.

6 ★ 🔊 42 **Listen to the conversation. What two ideas do Stella and Jason have? Why won't they do them?**

7 ★★★ 🔊 42 **Listen again and complete the conversation.**

Stella:	¹_____ in the Christmas holidays?
Jason:	What about skiing in the Pyrenees?
Stella:	Skiing? ²_____ go skiing, thank you!
Jason:	Why ?
Stella:	Because I can't ski … and neither can you!
Jason:	Oh yeah! … I forgot about that!
Stella:	³_____ New York?
Jason:	Yeah! That'll be nice. There's a lot to do there.
Stella:	We can go to museums, to the Statue of Liberty and we can go to a basketball match.
Jason:	Yes. ⁴_____ helicopter ride over Manhattan!
Stella:	Cool! That'll be amazing!
Jason:	OK, it'll be expensive. Do you think your parents will agree?
Stella:	Probably not. ⁵_____ ?
Jason:	I don't think so. Still, it was a good idea!

8 ★★ 🔊 42 **Listen again and check your answers. Then listen and repeat the conversation.**

Language focus extra

this, that, these, those

1 **Circle the correct words.**
1 (This) / Those is my house.
2 Those / That are Peter's shoes.
3 That / These is my mum.
4 These / This are my books.
5 This / Those are their friends.
6 That / Those is his bike.
7 These / This are our teachers.
8 Those / This is her laptop.

Possessive adjectives and possessive pronouns

2 (Circle) **the correct words.**
1 Ours / (Our) school is very big.
2 Their / Theirs names are Ruben and Lucia.
3 Your / Yours book is on the table.
4 His / Theirs sisters are nice.
5 Justin is five. His / Ours teacher is Mrs Milner.
6 Its / Yours name is The York School of English.

Possessive *'s*

3 **Add the possessive *'s* to the sentences.**
1 It is Susana*'s* skateboard.
2 This is my father car.
3 Put Pedro toys in the box.
4 This is my friend phone number.
5 She is Carlos mother.

4 **Put the words in the correct order to make sentences.**
1 are / friend's / my / These / headphones
These are my friend's headphones.
2 football / is / That / my / dog's

3 nice / sister's / friend / is / My

4 favourite / blue / Jack's / colour / is

5 uncle's / is / house / My / big

6 English / is / brother's / My / teacher

be: affirmative, negative and questions

5 **Write the sentences with contractions of the verb *be*.**
1 I am from Tokyo.
I'm from Tokyo.
2 It is midnight.

3 They are friends.

4 You are at school.

5 We are happy.

6 He is fourteen.

7 She is Turkish.

6 **Complete the sentences with the correct form of the verb *be*.**
1 The mouse ____*is*____ in the box. (✔)
2 The ruler _____ on the desk. (✗)
3 The pencils _____ next to the pencil sharpener. (✗)
4 We _____ in the classroom. (✔)
5 I _____ eighteen years old. (✗)
6 You _____ my friend. (✔)
7 He _____ from China. (✗)
8 She _____ English. (✔)
9 They _____ on the bus. (✗)

7 **Write questions for the sentences in Exercise 6. Answer them with short answers.**
1 *Is the mouse in the box?* _____*Yes, it is.*_____
2 _____ ?

3 _____ ?

4 _____ ?

5 _____ ?

6 _____ ?

7 _____ ?

8 _____ ?

9 _____ ?

Language focus extra

have got: affirmative and negative

1 Complete with the correct affirmative form of *have got*.

1 We ___*have got*___ long hair.
2 I _____ red trainers.
3 Andrew _____ two sisters.
4 Eric and Ernie _____ skateboards.
5 Our house _____ two bedrooms.
6 You _____ four books.

2 Write the sentences in the negative.

1 I've got a red rubber.
   I haven't got a red rubber.
2 Claudia has got a new games console.
   _____
3 They've got a blue car.
   _____
4 My dog has got a big nose.
   _____
5 We've got a new teacher.
   _____
6 He's got an MP3 player.
   _____

3 Write affirmative (✓) or negative (✗) sentences with *have got*.

1 She / two cousins   (✓)
   She's got two cousins.
2 I / blue eyes   (✓)
   _____
3 Harry / a pencil   (✗)
   _____
4 You / a bike   (✗)
   _____
5 Our house / a big garden   (✓)
   _____
6 My grandparents / mobile phones   (✗)
   _____

have got: questions and short answers

4 Use the information to write questions and short answers.

	Elisa	Rosie and Rob
brown hair	✓	✗
a cat	✗	✓
a comic	✓	✗

1 *Has Elisa got brown hair?*
   Yes, she has.
2 _____
   _____
3 _____
   _____
4 _____
   _____
5 _____
   _____
6 _____
   _____

Comparative adjectives

5 Write the comparative forms of the adjectives.

1 dark   ___*darker*___   5 young   _____
2 curly   _____   6 pretty   _____
3 intelligent _____   7 big   _____
4 beautiful   _____   8 thin   _____

6 Put the words in the correct order to make sentences.

1 me / Greg / intelligent / is / than / more
   Greg is more intelligent than me.
2 thinner / my / I / than / am / dad
   I _____
3 sister / curlier / has / My / mum / hair / my / got / than
   My sister _____
4 than / is / house / Our / bigger / our / garden
   Our garden _____
5 are / me / My / than / younger / friends
   My _____
6 prettier / mum / Your / is / than / sister / your
   Your sister _____

Language focus extra

Present simple: affirmative and negative

1 **Circle** the correct words.
1 Stella **have** / **has** breakfast at 7.30.
2 Tom and Steve **start** / **starts** school at 9.00.
3 We **do** / **does** our homework in the library.
4 Mr Thompson **give** / **gives** us a lot of homework.
5 School **finish** / **finishes** at 4.00.
6 I **speak** / **speaks** four languages.

2 **Complete the sentences with the correct form of the verbs in the box.**

> study   start   get   ~~live~~   go   teach

1 They _____live_____ in Moscow.
2 The class _____ at 6.30 pm.
3 I _____ dressed before breakfast.
4 We _____ shopping on Friday.
5 He _____ History at university.
6 His mum _____ at my school.

3 **Complete the sentences with the negative form of the verbs in bold.**
1 I __don't live__ in Madrid. I **live** in Barcelona.
2 He _____ lunch at school. He **has** lunch at home.
3 I **get up** early in the week, but I _____ early at the weekend.
4 Tom and his brother **like** football, but they _____ tennis.
5 Sarah _____ skateboarding in her garden. She **goes** skateboarding in the park.
6 You _____ basketball on Tuesday. You **play** basketball on Thursday.

4 **Rewrite the sentences. Use the information in brackets.**
1 Diana lives in Madrid. (Barcelona)
Diana doesn't live in Madrid. She lives in Barcelona.
2 We finish school at 4.00. (3.30)
_____
3 You go to dance classes on Tuesdays. (Art classes)
_____
4 They study Portuguese at their school. (French)
_____
5 His brother works in a bookshop. (supermarket)
_____
6 I play in the football team at school. (basketball)
_____

Adverbs of frequency

5 **Put the words in the correct order to make sentences.**
1 listen / They / to music / in the morning / always
They always listen to music in the morning.
2 usually / on / goes out / Patricia / Saturday
_____
3 late / Liz and Dave / are / often
_____
4 watch TV / morning / never / We / in / the
_____
5 happy / always / is / My dog
_____
6 sometimes / play / You / with your friends
_____

Present simple: *Yes/No* questions

6 **Circle** the correct words.
1 Do / **Does** Harry play basketball on Saturdays?
2 **Do** / Does you like pizza?
3 **Do** / Does Sarah and Beatrice study French?
4 **Do** / Does we go swimming on Tuesdays or Thursdays?
5 Do / **Does** your mobile phone play music?
6 Do / **Does** Linda play tennis with you after school?

7 **Write affirmative (✓) or negative (✗) short answers to the questions.**
1 Do they like football? (✗) *No, they don't.*
2 Does she do karate? (✓) _____
3 Do they live in England? (✗) _____
4 Do you like playing computer games? (✓) _____
5 Does Andrew study Art? (✗) _____
6 Do we finish at three o'clock? (✓) _____

Present simple: *Wh-* questions

8 **Complete the sentences with *do* or *does*.**
1 What time _____do_____ we go to dance class?
2 Where _____ Marimar live?
3 _____ you usually watch TV at night?
4 What time _____ your sister go to bed?
5 Who _____ she play with?
6 How often _____ you eat pizza?

Language focus extra

can for ability and permission

1 **Write sentences using can.**

1 Katie / watch TV
Katie can watch TV.

2 Jamie / run very fast
_____

3 Charlie and I / help you
_____

4 You / play on my games console
_____

5 My uncle / do karate
_____

6 I / go out with my friends
_____

2 **Write questions using can and the pronouns in brackets.**

1 I can swim. (you)
Can you swim?

2 He can play the guitar. (they)
_____

3 Jane can dance. (he)
_____

4 Alex can stay up late at the weekend. (we)
_____

5 We can watch TV after school. (she)
_____

6 They can use the computer. (I)
_____

3 **Write the sentences in the negative.**

1 John can play basketball.
John can't play basketball.

2 I can help them with their homework.
_____

3 She can do judo.
_____

4 Will and I can go to Mary's house.
_____

5 You can count to 50 in English.
_____

6 Sam can use your computer.
_____

4 **Use the information in the table to write questions and short answers.**

	Richard	Tim and Laura
paint well	✓	✗
use a computer	✗	✓
say the alphabet in English	✓	✗

1 *Can Richard paint well? Yes, he can.*
2 _____
3 _____
4 _____
5 _____
6 _____

(don't) like, don't mind, love, hate + ing

5 **Complete the sentences with the -ing form of the verbs in brackets.**

1 He loves ____*going*____ to school. (go)
2 I don't like _____ homework. (do)
3 Karen loves _____ DVDs. (watch)
4 We don't mind _____ English. (learn)
5 They don't like _____ pictures. (paint)
6 My brother hates _____ . (sing)

Object pronouns

6 **Circle the correct words.**

1 I like he / *him*.
2 She doesn't like **we** / **us**.
3 It's my favourite book. I love **it** / **him**.
4 I don't mind **she** / **her**, but she hates **me** / **I**.
5 I like your headphones. Can I use **they** / **them**?
6 I love that song. I can play **it** / **her** on the guitar.

7 **Complete the sentences with the object pronouns in the box.**

them   her   me   ~~us~~   it   him

1 Our teacher always tells _____*us*_____ to sit down.
2 It's a great film. Watch _____ !
3 She's got exams. She needs to study for _____ .
4 Alan goes to Art classes. I can go with _____ .
5 My cousin Katie knows the answer. I can email _____ tomorrow.
6 My best friend always tells _____ her secrets.

Language focus extra

Countable and uncountable nouns

1 Write *C* (countable) or *U* (uncountable) for the nouns in **bold**.

1 Can I have an **apple**?   *C*
2 I need four **carrots**.   ___
3 She has **milk** for breakfast.   ___
4 Tom has got two **bananas**.   ___
5 Evie loves **cheese**.   ___

2 Complete the table with the words.

> eggs   vegetables   milk   banana
> ice cream   water   sandwich   apple
> rice   carrot   meat   cheese

singular	plural	uncountable
	eggs	

3 Circle the correct words.

1 Can I have **a** / **an** sandwich, please?
2 We haven't got **some** / **any** bananas.
3 Has Sam got **a** / **any** milk in his packed lunch?
4 Take **some** / **a** water with you to school.
5 Do you want **an** / **any** apple?
6 Have we got **some** / **any** eggs?

4 Complete the sentences with *a/an*, *some* or *any*.

1 We've got _____*a*_____ red car.
2 I've got _____ bananas.
3 Ana doesn't like _____ rice.
4 Can I have _____ carrot, please?
5 They haven't got _____ vegetables.
6 Have you got _____ green pen?

there is / there are

5 Complete the sentences with *there is / there are* (✓) or *there isn't / there aren't* (✗).

1 ___*There isn't*___ any bread.   (✗)
2 _____ 28 students in my class.   (✓)
3 _____ a chair for me.   (✗)
4 _____ a dictionary on the table. (✓)
5 _____ some cheese sandwiches.   (✓)
6 _____ any books.   (✗)

6 Use the information to write questions and short answers about the two places.

	Hessle	Cottingham
a sports centre	✗	✓
good restaurants	✓	✗
a cinema	✗	✓

1 *Is there a sports centre in Hessle? No, there isn't.*
2 _____
3 _____
4 _____
5 _____
6 _____

7 Correct the incorrect sentences.

1 ~~Are~~ there a cinema in your town?
   Is there a cinema in your town?
2 There are some bananas in the cupboard.
   _____
3 There aren't some sandwiches.
   _____
4 Are there any vegetables for dinner?
   _____
5 There's a egg. Do you want it?
   _____
6 There are any pens in the pencil case.
   _____
7 There's some rice.
   _____
8 There's a apple on the tree.
   _____

much / many / a lot of

8 Complete the sentences with *much*, *many* or *a lot of*.

1 **A:** How ____*many*____ students are there in your class?
   B: There are 35.
2 **A:** How _____ cousins have you got?
   B: I've got nine cousins.
3 **A:** Has Jenny got any good DVDs?
   B: Yes, she's got _____ good DVDs.
4 There isn't _____ orange juice – only one bottle!
5 **A:** Are there any shops in your town?
   B: Yes, there are _____ shops.

Language focus extra

Present continuous: affirmative and negative

1 **Write the *-ing* form of the verbs.**

1 run ___running___ 4 play _____
2 help _____ 5 write _____
3 stop _____ 6 swim _____

2 **Complete the sentences with the present continuous form of the verbs in the box.**

> get   use   have   listen   write   ~~read~~   show

1 Joshua ____is reading____ the newspaper.
2 I _____ lunch. Can I telephone you this afternoon?
3 They _____ dressed to go out this evening.
4 She can't hear you. She _____ to music on her headphones.
5 The teacher _____ us some old photographs.
6 Dad _____ the computer. He _____ an email to Uncle Rob.

3 **Complete the sentences with the negative form of the present continuous. Remember to use contractions!**

1 You ___aren't listening___ to me! (listen)
2 Sally _____ football. (play)
3 We _____ the dog. (walk)
4 Joe and Chloe _____ to Sam. (speak)
5 I _____ at you! (laugh)
6 They _____ TV! (watch)

4 **Write affirmative and negative sentences in the present continuous.**

1 he / read / a comic (✓)
  He's reading a comic.
2 they / listen / to us (✗)
  _____
3 Laura / do / her homework (✓)
  _____
4 I / concentrate / on this exercise (✗)
  _____
5 we / go / to our Art class (✓)
  _____
6 Joe / eat / his lunch (✗)
  _____

Present continuous: questions and short answers

5 **Complete the questions and short answers.**

1 _Am_ I _helping_ ? (help)
  Yes, you are. (✓)
2 _____ he _____ (smile)
  _____ (✓)
3 _____ they _____ ? (dance)
  _____ (✗)
4 _____ we _____ in the race tomorrow? (run)
  _____ (✓)
5 _____ she _____ her teeth? (brush)
  _____ (✗)
6 _____ you _____ dinner with us? (have)
  _____ (✓)

Present continuous vs. present simple

6 **Complete the sentences with the present simple or present continuous.**

1 We ____go____ swimming at the sports centre on Friday. (go)
2 I _____ to the football on the radio. It's 2–1! (listen)
3 How often _____ you _____ your friends after school? (see)
4 _____ you _____ the homework? (understand)
5 It _____ , but I don't want to go out. (not rain)
6 I can't see you! Where _____ you _____ ? (hide)

7 **Choose the correct options.**

1 I ___ an email to my best friend.
  ⓐ am writing   **b** write
2 My grandma ___ to the zoo.
  a is never going   **b** never goes
3 Giraffes ___ for two hours every day.
  a are sleeping   **b** sleep
4 We ___ the bird of prey show at the moment.
  a are watching   **b** watch
5 Vicki ___ to the swimming pool in the summer.
  a is always going   **b** always goes
6 ___ that animal programme at the moment?
  a Are you watching   **b** Do you watch

Language focus extra

was/were

1 Circle the correct words.

1 She **was** / were here at 8 am.
2 We **wasn't** / **weren't** at the cinema.
3 Why **was** / **were** Jim and Daniel late?
4 I **was** / **were** at school yesterday.
5 Where **were** / **was** you at 9.30?
6 Tony **weren't** / **wasn't** happy.

2 Write questions with *was/were*. Answer them with short answers.

1 your dad / with you? (✗)
   Was your dad with you? No, he wasn't.

2 the film / good? (✓)
   _____

3 you / at home / at 8 pm? (✗)
   _____

4 the city centre / busy / on Saturday? (✓)
   _____

5 they / at the bowling alley / last night? (✓)
   _____

6 we / on holiday / in June? (✗)
   _____

3 Complete the questions with *was/were* and the question words in the box.

~~Why~~ Why Where What How much Who

1 ___Why were___ Adam and Joe at the shopping centre?
2 _____ you last night at 9 pm?
3 _____ the girl with short hair?
4 _____ the name of your first teacher?
5 _____ you happy this morning?
6 _____ the trainers at the market?

there was/were

4 Complete the text with the correct form of *there was/were*.

My granddad says that our town is very different now. Fifty years ago, ¹ _there were_ a lot of little shops, and ² _____ a big market every week, but ³ _____ any shopping centres! Where the big shopping centre is now, ⁴ _____ a nice park to walk in, but ⁵ _____ any museums for the tourists. It wasn't a problem. Granddad says that ⁶ _____ any tourists!

Past simple: regular and irregular verbs

5 Complete the sentences with the affirmative past simple form of the verbs in the box.

escape ~~walk~~ start live watch stay

1 We ___walked___ to school this morning.
2 The class _____ at 4.30.
3 Twenty years ago, my parents _____ in Edinburgh.
4 In the summer, we _____ at my grandparents' house for three weeks.
5 Last week, a lion _____ from the zoo.
6 Jake _____ TV all weekend.

6 Write the past simple of the verbs.

1 study ___studied___   4 see _____
2 get _____   5 do _____
3 stop _____   6 have _____

7 Put the letters in order and complete the sentences with irregular past simple forms.

1 She _____read_____ the book last summer. (erad)
2 We _____ swimming last weekend. (nwet)
3 I _____ a lot of animals in Australia. (wsa)
4 Emma and Frances _____ lunch with us. (dha)
5 My brother _____ up late this morning. (tgo)
6 You _____ four burgers! (tea)

ago

8 Put the words in the correct order to make sentences.

1 saw / two weeks / I / him / ago
   I saw him two weeks ago.

2 three years / stayed / Aunt Rachel / at my house / ago
   _____

3 the cup / ago / My football team / won / ten seasons
   _____

4 ago / my homework / did / half an hour / I
   _____

5 our class project / finished / We / ago / four days
   _____

Language focus extra

Past simple: *Yes/No* questions

1 **Write past simple questions.**

1 you / go shopping / yesterday?
Did you go shopping yesterday?

2 your parents / go / to a restaurant?

3 Ian / go cycling / in the park?

4 your brother / start school / last week?

5 their team / win the cup / last year?

6 you / see / Simon / on the TV / last night?

2 **Write the questions.**

1 Simon looked at the teacher.
Did Simon look at the teacher?

2 You put the milk in the fridge.

3 They got home very late.

4 Anthony liked the park.

5 I went to the shop.

6 Molly did her homework.

3 **This is what Alan, Hannah and Zoe did last weekend. Complete the table with answers about you, then use the information to write questions and short answers.**

	Alan	Hannah and Zoe	You
play computer games	✗	✓	
go shopping	✓	✗	

1 *Did Alan play computer games?*
No, he didn't.

2

3

4

5

6

Past simple: *Wh-* questions

4 **Match the beginnings and the ends of the questions.**

1 Where   a   like the museum?
2 What   b   did he get up?
3 Did she   c   did Olivia go?
4 What time   d   is your birthday?
5 How long   e   did you have for lunch?
6 When   f   did she need to do her homework?

5 **Order the words to make questions in the past simple.**

1 snowboarding / go / did / Where / you / ?
Where did you go snowboarding?

2 do / did / What / you / last night / ?

3 play / volleyball / they / did / When / ?

4 the match / lose / your team / Why / did / ?

5 basketball / play / you / did / What time / ?

6 with / did / you / Who / windsurfing / go / ?

Past simple: *Wh-* and *Yes/No* questions

6 **Write past simple questions.**

1 Why / give him / my comic / ?
Why did you give him my comic?

2 you / go out / last night / ?

3 What / they / have for dinner / ?

4 When / Jack / start school / ?

5 Where / she / go on holiday / ?

6 you / have / a good weekend / ?

Language focus extra

be going to: affirmative and negative

1 Write sentences using *be going to*.

1 They / go shopping on Saturday
They're going to go shopping on Saturday.

2 Andrew / phone me tonight
_____

3 I / play my favourite song
_____

4 You / watch a DVD
_____

5 My mum / help me
_____

6 We / ride our bikes
_____

2 Write the sentences in the negative.

1 Josh is going to tidy his bedroom.
Josh isn't going to tidy his bedroom.

2 I'm going to study Maths.
_____

3 Rebecca's going to get up early tomorrow.
_____

4 Carl and Simon are going to wear shorts.
_____

5 We're going to take our MP3 players.
_____

6 You're going to buy a new mobile phone.
_____

be going to: questions

3 Complete the questions with *be going to* and the verbs in the box. Answer them with short answers.

have   wear   ~~meet~~   study   go   help

1 _Are_ they _going to meet_ us at the cinema?
No, they aren't. (✗)

2 _____ you _____ a skirt?
_____ (✓)

3 _____ she _____ surfing?
_____ (✗)

4 _____ we _____ pizza?
_____ (✓)

5 _____ your brother _____ you?
_____ (✓)

6 _____ I _____ English today?
_____ (✗)

4 Write questions with *be going to*.

1 What time / Lily / arrive?
What time is Lily going to arrive?

2 Where / they / get married?
_____

3 How long / you / be on holiday?
_____

4 Why / Aiden / buy a new camera?
_____

5 What / you / wear to the party?
_____

6 When / it / stop raining?
_____

Future with *will/won't*

5 Complete the sentences with *will* or *won't* and the verbs in brackets.

1 I hope the weather ___*will be*___ (be) nice tomorrow.

2 Are you sure you _____ (come) to the party tonight?

3 Our team _____ (not win) the match on Saturday.

4 My dad says we _____ (not have) books in the future.

5 My grandfather says it _____ (be) cloudy tomorrow.

6 I think he _____ (meet) me at the bus stop.

7 Sheila hopes she _____ (see) some gorillas at the zoo.

6 Put the words in the correct order to make questions with *will*.

1 long / in / How / you / will / Dublin / be ?
How long will you be in Dublin?

2 tomorrow / it / Will / or rainy / be / sunny ?
_____

3 see / Tania / When / again / we / will ?
_____

4 sure / tomorrow / you / cycling / he / Are / won't / go ?
_____

5 do / university / study / you / What / you / at / will / think ?
_____

6 rice and / dinner / Frank / Will / eat / for / vegetables ?
_____

Thanks and acknowledgments

The authors and publishers would like to thank a number of people whose support has proved invaluable during the planning, writing and production process of this course.

We would like to thank Diane Nicholls for researching and writing the Get it Right pages, Alice Martin for writing the original Starter Unit, Ingrid Wisniewska for writing the original Review sections and Mick Green for writing the original Grammar Extra sections.

The authors and publishers are grateful to the following contributors:

Blooberry: concept design
emc design limited: text design and layouts
emc design limited: cover design
David Morritt and Ian Harker - DSound: audio recordings
Corpus

Development of this publication has made use of the Cambridge English Corpus (CEC). The CEC is a computer database of contemporary spoken and written English, which currently stands at over one billion words. It includes British English, American English and other varieties of English. It also includes the Cambridge Learner Corpus, developed in collaboration with the University of Cambridge ESOL Examinations. Cambridge University Press has built up the CEC to provide evidence about language use that helps to produce better language teaching materials.

The publishers are grateful to the following for permission to reproduce copyright photographs and material:

p. 4 (L2): Shutterstock Images/kuppa; p. 4 (L4): Shutterstock Images/gillmar; p. 4 (L5): Shutterstock Images/mhatzapa; p. 4 (L7): Shutterstock Images/rangizzz; p. 4 (R1): Shutterstock Images/Alexlukin; p. 4 (R1): Shutterstock Images/Picsfive; p. 4 (R3): Shutterstock Images/zirconicusso; p. 4 (R6): Alamy/©Kirsty Pargeter; p. 5 (1): Shutterstock Images/artjazz; p. 5 (2): Alamy/©Nikreates; p. 9 (1A): Alamy/©Beyond Fotomedia GmbH; p. 9 (1B): Alamy/©RubberBall; p. 9 (1C): Superstock/RubberBall; p. 9 (BL): Getty/Michel Dufour/French Select; p. 9 (BL): Rex Features/Startraks Photo; p. 9 (BR): Alamy/©AlamyCelebrity; p. 9 (BR): Rex Features/Broadimage; p. 9 (BCL): Unimedia Images/Rex Features; p. 9 (BCR): Alamy/©Nippon News Aflo Co. Ltd.; p. 11 (T): Shutterstock Images/Rene Jansa; p. 11 (C): Corbis/Cheque; p. 11 (B): Alamy/©National Geographic Image Collection; p. 12 (T): Shutterstock Images/s_bukley; p. 17 (TR): Getty/Louis-Paul St-Onge/E+; p. 18 (T): Shutterstock Images/Hans Kim; p. 18 (B): Getty/Adrianna Williams/The Image Bank; p. 21 (1): Alamy / Lucianne Pashley/age fotostock; p. 21 (2): Shutterstock Images/Denis Kuvaev; p. 21 (3): SuperStock/Pictures Ltd; p. 21 (4): Alamy/©Janine Wiedel Photolibrary; p. 21 (5): Shutterstock Images/Marijus Auruskevicius; p. 21 (6): Shutterstock Images/Vvoe; p. 21 (A): Alamy/©Mixa; p. 21 (B): Shutterstock Images/Best Photo Studio; p. 21 (C): Alamy/©Rob Lewine/Tetra Images; p. 21 (D): Shutterstock Images/Vadim Kozlovsky; p. 22 (C): Shutterstock Images/Andresr; p. 27 (1): Alamy/©Andrew Fox; p. 27 (2): Alamy/©VIEW Pictures Ltd; p. 27 (3): Alamy/©redsnapper; p. 27 (4): Alamy/©Mike Booth; p. 27 (5): Alamy/©Janine Wiedel Photolibrary; p. 27 (6): Alamy/©Archimage; p. 27 (7): Alamy/©Andrew Aitchison; p. 27 (8): Alamy/©Peter Titmuss; p. 29 (TL): Alamy/©Megapress; p. 31 (T): Shutterstock Images/BasPhoto; p. 31 (CL): Corbis/Peter Dench/In Pictures; p. 31 (CR): Alamy/©TravelStockCollection – Homer Sykes; p. 31 (B): Corbis/Peter Dench/In Pictures; p. 32 (TR): Alamy/©MBI; p. 32 (L): Corbis/Richard Hutchings; p. 37 (1): Alamy/©John James; p. 37 (2): Shutterstock Images/Robyn Mackenzie; p. 37 (3): Shutterstock Images/Viktor; p. 37 (4): Rex Features/organic Picture Library; p. 37 (5): Shutterstock Images/Multiart; p. 37 (6): Shutterstock Images/MaraZe; p. 37 (7): Shutterstock Images/Olga_Phoenix; p. 37 (8): Shutterstock Images/Larina Natalia; p. 37 (9): Alamy/©Libby Welch; p. 37 (10): Shutterstock Images/TAGSTOCK1; p. 38 (TC): Shutterstock Images/John Wynn; p. 38 (R): Alamy/©Svetlana Foote; p. 38 (BC): Alamy/©foodfolio; p. 38 (L): Shutterstock Images/Maks Narodenko; p. 38 (CR): Alamy/©Hera Food; p. 39 (1): Shutterstock Images/Foodiepics; p. 39 (2): Shutterstock Images/John Wynn; p. 39 (3): Shutterstock Images/Timmary; p. 39 (4): Shutterstock Images/Malivan_Iuliia; p. 39 (5): Shutterstock Images/Jill Chen; p. 39 (6): Shutterstock Images/Marco Mayer; p. 39 (7): Shutterstock Images/mylisa; p. 39 (8): Shutterstock Images/ronstik; p. 39 (CL): Alamy/©Science Photo Library;

p. 39 (CC): Shutterstock Images/East; p. 39 (CR): Shutterstock Images/Indigo Fish; p. 39 (BL): Shutterstock Images/ElenaGaak; p. 39 (BC): Shutterstock Images/farbled; p. 39 (BR): Shutterstock Images/Brent Hofacker; p. 41 (B/G): Getty/Juan Silva/The Image Bank; p. 41 (T): Alamy/©Foodcollection.com; p. 41 (R): Superstock/Tips Images; p. 42 (TR): Alamy/©Roger Cracknell 10/Pagan Festivals; p. 42 (TCR): Superstock/©Hackenberg/F1 ONLINE; p. 42 (CR): Shutterstock Images/Lucia Pescaru; p. 42 (BC): Shutterstock Images/O.Bellini; p. 42 (L): Alamy/©Carine Vaissiere; p. 42 (BR): Shutterstock Images/Petr Jilek; p. 46 (center): Maskot/Glowimages; p. 48 (L1): Alamy/©Sarah Peters/imagebroker; p. 48 (L2): Getty/ranplett/Vetta; p. 48 (L3): Superstock/Science Photo Library; p. 48 (L4): Alamy/©kpzfoto; p. 48 (L5): Shutterstock Images/andamanec; p. 48 (L6): Superstock/Tips Images; p. 49 (1): Shutterstock Images/Naypong; p. 49 (2): Shutterstock Images/Kachalkina Veronika; p. 49 (3): Shutterstock Images/Donjiy; p. 49 (4): Alamy/©Chris Mattison; p. 49 (5): Shutterstock Images/neelsky; p. 49 (6): Shutterstock Images/jadimages; p. 49 (7): Shutterstock Images/defpicture; p. 49 (8): Shutterstock Images/Jordan Tan; p. 49 (9): Shutterstock Images/M.M.; p. 49 (10): Alamy/©Top-Pet-Pics; p. 50 (L): Alamy/©Dallas and John Heaton/Travel Pictures; p. 50 (C): Alamy/©David Cantrille; p. 50 (R): Getty/David Wall Photo/Lonely Planet Images; p. 51 Alamy/©ZUMA Press, Inc.; p. 52 (C): Shutterstock Images/Steve Mann; p. 53 (R): Shutterstock Images/SasPartout; p. 53 (B): Shutterstock Images/photobar; p. 56: (C) Alamy/©Arvidas Saladauskas; p. 57 (1): Getty/Atlantide S.N.C./age footstock; p. 57 (2): Alamy/©Aardvark; p. 57 (3): Alamy/©Marc Macdonald; p. 57 (4): Alamy/©Stephen Dorey ABIPP; p. 57 (5): Alamy/©PBimages; p. 57 (6): Alamy/©Greg Balfour Evans; p. 57 (7): Alamy/©eye35.pix; p. 57 (8): Shutterstock Images/Tischenko Irina; p. 58 (L): Alamy/©AJSenviron; p. 58 (R): Alamy/©photosilta; ; p. 60 (B): Shutterstock Images/David W Hughes; p. 61 (CL): Alamy/©Rob Ford; p. 61 (BL): Alamy/©Ian Macpherson London; p. 61 (L): Alamy/©Eric Nathan; p. 62 (T): Getty/Dan Porges/Peter Arnold; p. 62 (C): Alamy/©kpzfoto; p. 62 (B): Shutterstock Images/Jacek Chabraszewski; p. 65 (R): Alamy/©GlowImages; p. 67 (1): Corbis/BERTHIER Emmanuel/Hemis; p. 67 (2): Alamy/©PictureNet Corporation; p. 67 (3): Shutterstock Images/oliveromg; p. 67 (5): Corbis/Chris Cole/Duomo; p. 67 (7): Shutterstock Images/Jacek Chabraszewski; p. 67 (4): Getty/technotr/E+; p. 67 (6): Shutterstock Images/Petrenko Andriy; p. 67 (8): Getty/Mike Kemp; p. 67 (9): Shutterstock Images/tammykayphoto; p. 68 (TL): Shutterstock Images/Felix Mizioznikov; p. 68 (TR): Radius Images / Alamy; p. 68 (BR): Shutterstock Images/Kzenon; p. 69 (R): Superstock/Antoine Juliette/Oredia/Oredia Eurl; p. 70 (B): Shutterstock Images/Mike Liu; p. 71 (L): Getty/Richard Bouhet/AFP; p. 71 (B): Corbis/Carlos De Saa/epa; p. 72 (C): Shutterstock Images/almonfoto; p. 72 (CR): Alamy/©epa european pressphoto agency b.v.; p. 72 (TR): Alamy/©ZUMA Press; Inc.; p. 75 (BR): Alamy/©Dennis MacDonald; p. 76 (right): Alamy/©Frances Roberts; p. 79 (R): Superstock/Alaska Stock; p. 80 (BL): Getty/Andy Stothert/Britain On View; p. 80 (BC): Shutterstock Images/FooTToo; p. 80 (BR): Alamy/©Pascal Broze/ONOKY – Photononstop; p. 81 (TL): Superstock/Travel Library Limited; p. 81 (TR): Alamy/©David Wall; p. 81 (BL): Alamy/©Image Source Plus; p. 81 (BR): Shutterstock Images/Waj; p. 82 (TR): Shutterstock Images/Ammit Jack; p. 82 (C): Superstock/Stefano Paterna/age fotostock; p. 85 (TR): Shutterstock Images/karamysh; p. 87 (BL): OtnaYdur/Shutterstock Images; p. 87 (BL): ONOKY - Photononstop/Alamy; p. 87 (BL): Luminis/Shutterstock Images; p. 88 (B): Cusp/Superstock; p. 88 (C): vvoe/Shutterstock Images; p. 89 (BL): Ableimages/Superstock; p. 89 (BR): Marmaduke St. John/Alamy; p. 90 (C): Blend Images/Shutterstock Images; p. 91 (CR): Masterfile; p. 91 (BL): incamerastock/Alamy; p. 92 (BL): jon challicom/Alamy; p. 92 (TR): Andres Rodriguez/Alamy; p. 93 (BL): Jason Kasumovic/Shutterstock Images; p. 93 (BR): AGIF/Shutterstock Images; p. 94 (BL): Radius Images/Alamy; p. 94 (TR): Songquan Deng/Shutterstock.

The publishers are grateful to the following illustrators:

David Belmonte (Beehive Illustration): p. 4 (L), 5 (TR), 7, 8, 9, 24, 28 (BL), 40 (TR), 44, 54; Anni Betts: p. 49, 59 (L); Emmanuel Cerisier (Beehive Illustration): p. 14, 78, 84; Russ Cook: p. 3 (CL), 30; Alberto de Hoyos: p. 29, 59 (R), 60, 64; Nigel Dobbyn (Beehive Illustration): p. 4 (R), 6, 16, 34, 47; Mark Draisey: p. 25, 28 (TL), 48 (TR), 57, 74 (TR); Mark Duffin: p. 69, 77; Q2A Media Inc.: p. 5 (3, 4, 5, 6); Jose Rubio: p. 10, 48 (BR); Dave Russell: 5 (BL), 15, 79; David Shephard (Bright Agency): p. 3 (BL, R), 17, 19, 40 (L), 74 (BL).